5-MINUTE
ENERGY

5-MINUTE
ENERGY

A More Vibrant, Engaged, and Purposeful You
in Just 5 MINUTES A DAY

ISADORA BAUM

Adams Media
New York London Toronto Sydney New Delhi

Adams Media
An Imprint of Simon & Schuster, Inc.
57 Littlefield Street
Avon, Massachusetts 02322

First Adams Media trade paperback edition October 2018

ADAMS MEDIA and colophon are trademarks of Simon & Schuster.

For information about special discounts for bulk purchases, please contact Simon & Schuster Special Sales at 1-866-506-1949 or business@simonandschuster.com.

The Simon & Schuster Speakers Bureau can bring authors to your live event. For more information or to book an event contact the Simon & Schuster Speakers Bureau at 1-866-248-3049 or visit our website at www.simonspeakers.com.

Interior design by Michelle Kelly

Manufactured in the United States of America

10 9 8 7 6 5 4 3 2 1

Library of Congress Cataloging-in-Publication Data
Baum, Isadora, author.
5-minute energy / Isadora Baum.
Avon, Massachusetts: Adams Media, 2018.
Series: 5-minute.
LCCN 2018023272 (print) | LCCN 2018024831 (ebook) | ISBN 9781507208823 (pb) | ISBN 9781507208830 (ebook)
Subjects: LCSH: Self-actualization (Psychology) | Stress management. | BISAC: SELF-HELP / Stress Management. | SELF-HELP / Personal Growth / Success.
Classification: LCC BF637.S4 (ebook) | LCC BF637 .S4 B388 2018 (print) | DDC 155.9/042--dc23
LC record available at https://lccn.loc.gov/2018023272

ISBN 978-1-5072-0882-3
ISBN 978-1-5072-0883-0 (ebook)

CONTENTS

INTRODUCTION 13

PART 1
Energize Your Life 15

Say "I Love You" Each Day 16
Stay On Your Feet 17
Keep a Gratitude Journal 19
Stock Up on Snacks! 21
Let Music In 23
Take a Deep Breath 24
Try Something New! 25
Hit Up a HIIT Workout 26
Make Someone Laugh 27
Smile 28
Stretch Your Limbs 29
Read a Poem 31
Get Outside! 32
Meditate! 34
Make a Dream List 36

Tidy Up! 37
Read the Paper 39
Practice a New Hobby 40
Sing Loud and Proud 41
Compliment Yourself! 42
Donate to a Charity 44
Eat Whole Grains 45
Embrace the Water 47
Stay Hydrated! 48
Get Cooking! 49
Have Mealtime with Family 50
Get Rid of Toxic Elements 51
Be Open to Love 53
Eat Mindfully 55
Ditch the Sugar 57
Eat Enough Iron 59
Don't Sweat the Small Stuff 61
Take a Probiotic 62
Don't Forget about Prebiotics . . .64
Channel Your Inner Yogi 66
Consider a "What If" Scenario . . .68

Touch Someone Gently 70
Take a Photo of Your Pet 71
Look for Cloud Art! 72
Pour a Glass of Wine 73
Forgive Yourself. 74
Indulge!. 75

PART 2
Energize Your Mind. 77

Think Positively!. 78
Take an Online Quiz 79
Try Mindfulness Meditation 81
Solve a Puzzle! 83
Learn a Few New Words! 84
Strike Up a Conversation with a
    Stranger 85
Chew Peppermint Gum 86
Take On Tree Pose. 87
Doodle!. 88
Rub Your Temples 89
Recite Powerful Words 90
Practice Positive Affirmation 91
Do a Visualization Technique 92
Try Self-Hypnosis 94
Share What You Love about
    Someone 96
Write a Personal Letter 97
Snap Your Fingers! 98
Scream!. 99
Pull Your Hair. 100
Get Excited!. 101
List Five Things You Love
    about Yourself 102
Pull Up a Favorite Social Media
    Account. 104
Get Engaged in Social Media! . . 105
Wet Your Eyes. 106
Color! 107
Knit!. 108
Play an Instrument. 109
Eat Something Fishy. 110
Sniff Ginger 112
Sit in Child's Pose 114
Do a Plank. 115
Go Into Downward Facing Dog . . 117
Touch Your Toes! 118
Play a Home Movie 119
Go Into Camel Pose 120
Share an Accomplishment with
    Someone 121
Share an Adventure! 122
Look in the Mirror! 123
Check In with an Old Friend 124
Set a Short-Term Goal. 125
Set a Long-Term Goal 126
Work On a Bad Habit. 127

Indulge in a Talent. 128
Pick Up a Magazine You've Never
    Read Before. 129
Ask Someone to List Your Good
    Qualities 131

PART 3
Energize Your Morning 133

Wake Up with a Few Breaths 134
Fix Your Hair 135
Drink Warm Water and Lemon. . .136
Set a Positive Intention 137
Stretch Your Neck 138
Power Up with Protein. 139
Say "Good Morning"
    to Someone. 141
Drink Some Coffee! 142
Get Your Heart Rate Up 144
Wink at Yourself. 145
Hop in the Shower 146
Make a To-Do List. 147
Think of Something That
    Scares You 148
Set Your Alarm to a Song. 149
Have a Green Juice! 150
Have a Shot of Apple
    Cider Vinegar 152

Eat Greek Yogurt. 153
Give Lox Some Love. 154
Make Plans! 155
Book an Exercise Class 156
Do Jumping Jacks. 157
Check Your Mailbox! 158
Brush Your Teeth 159
Gargle with Water. 160
Eat a Banana 161
Enjoy Your Commute 162
Eat Grapefruit! 164
Take a Photo of the Outdoors . . .165
Water the Plants 166
Eat an Apple 167
Have a Shot of Matcha 168
Clean Your Ears! 169
Spray Perfume or Cologne 170
Snap a Selfie 171
Drink a Smoothie. 172
Eat Espresso Beans 174
Give Someone a Kiss 175
Indulge in Some Wishful
    Thinking. 176
Stretch Your Feet. 177
Sip Kombucha! 179
Make Your Bed 180
Use the Restroom 181
Start Dinner. 182

PART 4

Energize Your Afternoon **183**

Take the Stairs! 184
Take a Brisk Walk........... 186
Splash Cool Water on
  Your Face 187
Practice a Power Pose........ 188
Inhale Essential Oils.......... 190
Drink a Glass of Cold Water.....192
Chat with a Coworker 193
Do Squats................ 194
Grab a Handful of Nuts 196
Write a Haiku.............. 198
Eat Some Fruit! 199
Pinch Yourself............. 201
Wash Your Hands 202
Hold Your Breath........... 203
Stretch Your Ankles 204
Look Up a Restaurant Menu....206
Text a Friend 207
Clean Your Glasses 208
Scratch Your Back.......... 210
Eat Something Salty.......... 211
Stretch Your Back 213
Open Up Your Hips 215
Take a Call While Pacing....... 217
Rotate Your Wrists 218
Pat Yourself on the Back 219

Give Yourself a Massage 220
Pat Someone Else on
  the Shoulder 221
Practice Kanban............ 222
Bite Your Tongue............ 224
Squeeze a Stress Ball 225
Bob Your Head to a Song 226
Whistle!................. 227
Stick Your Head Out
  the Window............. 228
Jump Rope 229
Wear Red!............... 230
Make a Yes/Meh List......... 231
Do a Wall Sit 233

PART 5

Energize Your Evening........235

Dance When Making Dinner ...236
Eat a Healthy Meal 237
Clean Something in Your Home . 239
Make Time for Sex.......... 240
Prep for Tomorrow 242
Dine with Good Company 243
Watch Your Favorite TV Show . 244
Indulge in Dark Chocolate! 245
Use a Foam Roller 246
Wash Your Face! 247

Cross Off Your To-Do List 248
Take Your Dog for a Walk. 249
Watch the Sun Set. 250
Swing a Kettlebell 251
Stare at Your Partner
    in Silence 253
Put the Phone on
    Airplane Mode. 254
Turn Down the Thermostat! 255
Light a Candle. 256
Look at a Photograph 257
Floss! 258
Take Out or Wet
    Your Contacts 259
Plant Something 260
Try Group Therapy 261
Wash the Dishes 263
Do Tabata. 264
Lift Weights. 266
Pick Out Your Outfit
    for Tomorrow 267
Scrub Yourself with a Loofah . . . 268
Take Out the Trash 269
Make a Random Plan
    after Work 270
Do Work You've Been
    Putting Off. 272
Play a Game of Cards 273
Try a New Food for Dinner 274

Ice Your Muscles 276
Have a Little Bit of Ice Cream. . . 277

INDEX 279

DEDICATION

I dedicate this book to you, the reader—someone searching for vibrancy and adventure, a dreamer who values hope and instinct and knows that the right kind of energy and outlook can turn those "what ifs" into a much-deserved reality. You have the power to seize the energy you want and follow your heart—channel it, use it to its fullest, and see where it leads you.

ACKNOWLEDGMENTS

I'd like to thank Simon & Schuster, as well as my educators, friends, and family who have supported my endeavors and believed in me for all these years. My mother is my biggest hero. She is my rock, my light, my source of inspiration—a courageous, ambitious, and *energetic* woman who offers so much positivity, playfulness, and love to those around her. For someone who's naturally expressive with words, I am at a loss in fully describing just how grateful I am, as I wouldn't be where I am today without her by my side. I love you, Mom.

INTRODUCTION

Maybe you're used to waking up still tired, feeling that slump in the middle of the day, or being drained by the time you get home at night. Fortunately, *5-Minute Energy* is here to help!

In this book you'll find more than two hundred energy-boosting activities organized by time of day, with some that you can do anytime at all! Some activities—like engaging in unexpected hobbies or trying new foods—may push you out of your comfort zone. Others—like drinking a glass of cold water or doing jumping jacks—may feel more familiar. But no matter what you choose to do, these activities will instantly energize your body, your mind, or both—all in just 5 minutes or less! These quick and easy energizing activities will also help you spark change, make a difference, and better your life—and the lives of others. They will give you the energy you need to live the best life possible!

Just remember, you never know which sources will wake you up and get you back in the game until you try them. So open this book to any page, and enjoy the burst of energy!

PART 1
ENERGIZE YOUR LIFE

SAY "I LOVE YOU" EACH DAY

There's no greater energizer than the support and love you get from your close friends and family! By knowing you are connected to others—those who similarly need you and rely on you for protection and care—you're given a purpose to take action and make life worthwhile, which leads to greater happiness, fulfillment, and well-being. Saying "I love you" not only makes the other person feel loved, but it also reminds you to build and cherish your relationships. With this energy, you are compelled to live life to its fullest, honoring those you love.

It's easy to express your thoughts even if you can't be face-to-face, as there are many ways to communicate in today's modern, tech-savvy world. Send a quick text message to a parent, friend, or partner, or give someone a call. Better yet? You can videochat via a service like *FaceTime* or *Skype* if you can't meet in person and still want that visual aspect.

STAY ON YOUR FEET

The body thrives off movement. Not only does staying active better your ticker, but it also improves your circulation, getting your blood flowing throughout your limbs! By keeping yourself busy, you're torching more calories effortlessly (get this: standing burns more calories than sitting!), and you're keeping your energy levels high and stable. Of course, this doesn't mean you need to be—or should be—spending hours and hours at the gym. It's more of a lifestyle adjustment in terms of being on your feet for a good portion of the day in order to have consistent blood flow and vitality. Here are a few—fun!—ways to get moving:

1. **Give yourself a dance break.** Pull up a song from your favorite playlist and bust out a few dance moves (in public or private, of course) for 5 minutes. You can repeat this throughout the day when you notice your energy draining—this little bit of movement will be an instant refresher.
2. **Count your steps.** Many apps, watches, and other gadgets can track your total number of steps for the day, so even if you can't squeeze in a workout, you can still figure out how many steps you walked, how many calories you burned, and what distance you've trekked during the day—all of which will add up to provide an adequate workout and supply energy. Set a goal for yourself, and work to get better and better over time.

3. **Get up from your chair.** Stuck in a sedentary job? At the computer all day? You can still take 5 minutes to stretch those legs, grab a new cup of coffee, take a pee break, or strike up a conversation with a coworker at the opposite end of the hall. Getting even just a little bit of movement in your legs will create a burst of energy that will travel throughout your body. And once you return to your desk, you'll be way more productive.

KEEP A GRATITUDE JOURNAL

Keep a journal, notebook, or diary by your bedside, and create a daily ritual where you list three or more things you are grateful for. This can be done twice daily, morning and night, where you express a few things you appreciate in general in the morning and three new things you appreciated that exact day in the evening. Or you can practice once, choosing a time that's most convenient for you.

By keeping a gratitude journal, you can remind yourself each morning and night of the wonderful aspects of your life and how they improve your well-being and happiness. Once you get into the groove, you'll notice that these 5 minutes can make you a happier, more energized person who's excited to embark on whatever journey life brings. Reflecting on how fortunate you've been so far will further increase your vigor for living each minute to its fullest and will encourage you to find new ways to appreciate the beauty and joy in life. There are so many future experiences to look forward to!

Even if you've had a bad day or a dip in energy levels, consider all that you should be grateful for—there are probably quite a few things worth jotting down. Think about your social network of friends and family; your successes, whether from work, personal hobbies and passions, or self-improvement; and even small, trivial things that can instantly make a day *that* much better. A smile from a stranger on the street? The smell of fresh laundry after you run a load? A favorite muffin available at your local coffee shop? There's so much good around you to take in.

Once you have your journal, you can decide who you'd like to share it with—if anyone. It can be private, for your eyes only, or you can reach out to those who are mentioned within and share an entry to boost their moods and energy states too. Gratitude can benefit everyone involved, so as long as you're okay with opening up and being vulnerable, you're sure to put a big, radiant smile on someone else's face—and that feels pretty *darn* good, right?

STOCK UP ON SNACKS!

When it comes to keeping your energy levels high, you need to provide your body with the right amount and kind of fuel. If you don't eat enough, or if you opt for foods that lack nutrition, it'll be hard to stay focused throughout the day or combat those dreaded afternoon lulls. Plus, if you are looking to exercise, you'll definitely need a snack beforehand to power your body through your full workout.

What to Eat?

- **Roasted beans:** These protein- and fiber-rich snacks boost energy levels by speeding up your metabolism! A sluggish metabolism can lead to lethargy, so you want to keep it running as well as you can. Plus, roasted beans are easy to store at the office or take on the go in zip-top bags. You can try broad beans, chickpeas, or edamame, and you can experiment with flavors, such as black pepper, sriracha, or wasabi.
- **Nuts:** A handful of nuts or a spread of nut butter on a slice of whole-grain bread can quickly banish fatigue and replenish energy stores. Choose from classic peanut or almond butter, or venture into new territory with hazelnut, cashew, and even macadamia nut butter.
- **Fruit and yogurt:** Pairing a bit of protein and carbs is a good way to keep energy stable, and you can easily store yogurt in an office

fridge. Try Greek yogurt for more benefits (gut-friendly bacteria and probiotic properties), and add some berries or banana slices for a punch of flavor!

- **Avocado toast:** Avocados are high in magnesium, which provides energy and helps you de-stress. Plus, they're high in fiber and healthy fats, so you'll stay fuller longer and keep your brain and body focused on tasks at hand. Get some whole-wheat or whole-grain bread rather than white bread, which can suck your energy. Whole grains offer complex carbohydrates that will better your brain and promote satiety. Together avocado and toast make the ultimate snack break!

Snacking on these foods will keep your energy levels stable during the day and will give you the right type of nourishment to feed both your mind and body.

LET MUSIC IN

Nothing says feel-good like an upbeat tune! So whenever you're starting to get tired or notice your eyes glazing over, look to one of your favorite jams to reset the mood. You can even dance along!

Customize an energy playlist that you can keep on hand—that way, when you're short on time or on the go, you can easily access it in a matter of seconds. You can create a mix, blending today's latest hits with a few happy classics and show tunes that never seem to get old or that bring up great memories. Use whatever music resonates with you. The more meaningful the song, the more mood-lifting it'll be. You really can't go wrong here, as music can enhance life satisfaction in general.

Once you've chosen your music, give yourself 5 minutes to really let the songs speak to your soul and get your energy levels pumping!

TAKE A DEEP BREATH

You may be surprised to learn that something so simple as breathing can actually have an empowering effect on the body and mind, but it's true! Breathing can instantly energize your body and help you regain clarity of thought, right when your attention span is dwindling and you're feeling fatigued.

When you breathe in and out, you let fresh air enter your body to bring about energy and balance that will ground you and help you focus. The fresh oxygen you get with each inhale will boost circulation, which in turn energizes the body and creates more space in the lungs. Breath work can also be helpful during times when you're anxious, as it can be very stabilizing for the mind and body. You can do this wherever you are—at work, at home, in the bathroom. It doesn't matter! This activity will stay with you no matter where you go! To get started, simply follow these steps:

1. Inhale to the count of two
2. Exhale to the count of two
3. Inhale to the count of two
4. Exhale to the count of three

And so forth. The exhales go up by one, as the inhales stay the same. You can do this for 5 minutes, and it'll move that fresh oxygen supply throughout your veins for greater energy stores.

TRY SOMETHING NEW!

The best way to maintain energy during the day? Shock the body and mind with surprise. When things become too mundane or you're stuck in a rut, it's easy to lose stamina. And that's a shame, since boredom and predictability can take you away from enjoying even the small, ordinary aspects of the day and can even compromise your abilities at work. After all, mental fog doesn't do deadlines and presentations any good!

The solution? Work in bits of novelty throughout the day, and invigorate your life:

- Try a different coffee shop, or order a drink you've never tried before.
- Put a surprise ingredient or spice in your cooking for a new take on a staple recipe.
- Leave your playlist behind and listen to a random song or two during your workout.
- Drive home on a different route to see new buildings and sites.
- Try a new self-care product, such as a perfume or bodywash. Spritz and smell something unfamiliar that can give you newfound energy.

These are just a few examples, but you should feel free to make up your own. And in fact, you really don't even need to plan these things in advance. They are more likely to energize you if they happen naturally, so seize the opportunity to experience something new and exciting and to boost those energy levels!

HIT UP A HIIT WORKOUT

HIIT is high-intensity interval training, and it is often incorporated into CrossFit, circuit training, and boot camp classes. It will spike your heart rate and energy levels by challenging you to do a lot of hard work in a short period of time. This type of workout is not for the faint of heart, so before heading into this high-intensity class, you should check with a physician to make sure it's safe based on your medical history and condition. If you're given the green light, you won't find a better, more energizing workout!

HIIT has been shown to burn tons of calories by blending both strength and cardio, and it can get your heart rate skyrocketing—especially when there's loud, upbeat music to go with it.

When you're taking your body to its limits and working at your greatest potential in a short amount of time, it's impossible *not* to finish drenched in sweat and with a renewed sense of vigor. I mean, you just *crushed* it. What's more energizing than that? Check for local gyms that offer HIIT classes and try one out. Then, you can do a 5-minute HIIT workout whenever you're in need of that quick energy boost. Pretty soon you'll be dreaming about burpees in your sleep!

MAKE SOMEONE LAUGH

There's no greater gift than laughter, and both you and the one you make laugh will wake up! How does laughter boost energy? Well, it instantly alerts you to your current situation, and it elicits an enthusiastic response in the form of a laugh. It also lowers the stress hormone cortisol, which has been shown to zap energy and increase negativity. Plus, if something's really funny and you can't help but giggle, it's a welcome break from whatever had been draining your energy stores. Of course, laughter comes in all forms, so go with whatever you think fits, based on the recipient's personality or whatever the moment brings.

You could share a humorous story about your day, tell a joke (a good "dad joke" never hurts, right?), or share a funny link or meme on the Internet through social media. In any case, knowing that you've put a grin on someone else's face will plant an equally bright one on yours as well, and you'll notice your energy go way up.

SMILE

Research has shown that smiling can improve your energy levels in a matter of seconds, simply due to the upturned grin itself. Even if you are in a bad mood, as long as you force a smile, you'll inevitably experience an energy burst and feel a bit better. Of course, that won't last for too long, so it's up to you to then figure out what steps to take to prolong the boost.

Here's a tip: when smiling, take 5 minutes and imagine something inspirational and stimulating as well—something that can wake you up and take you to a place and time where you were feeling great, with loved ones, or on your feet and taking action. Any of these scenarios will translate into a peppier state and zest for life. Think of this as a montage of happy thoughts and moments moving through your mind.

So simply smile, think happy thoughts, maybe let out a laugh or two, and reap the benefits!

STRETCH YOUR LIMBS

When your body is stagnant and blood circulation is at a low, you're likely going to see your energy levels plummet, since your body isn't being used effectively to generate energy and get fresh blood flowing through your limbs. You don't want blood to pool at a point like your ankles, as it takes away that source of vitality your brain needs to stay awake and focused. The mind and the body are more alert when there's steady circulation, and a lack of oxygenated blood supply to the brain can lead to fatigue and lack of concentration. A solution? Get up out of your chair and do some stretches, which can provide a boost in circulation and get more oxygenated blood to different parts of the body. These are the areas you should target:

1. **The neck:** Gently tilt your head to stretch your neck to the left, and hold for 2 seconds. Bring it back to the center, and hold it upright for 5 seconds. Then gently tilt your head to the right, holding for 2 seconds again. For an extra stretch, lightly pull your head to each side. Start with your right hand lightly touching your head, then lean your neck toward your right shoulder. Then switch hands and repeat on your left side.

2. **The back:** Lift your arms overhead and lock your hands together with your palms facing inward. Extend your arms outward behind you to stretch your back. Then, extending your arms behind your

back even farther, stick your chest out and stay upright and tall, with good posture. Then bring your body down so your eyes are looking at your toes and your head is loose, looking downward. Finally, unlock your hands and bring your arms in front of your body. Let your hands cradle your elbows in front of you and rock back and forth ever so slowly.

3. **The legs:** First, shake out those legs. Then spread them apart, sinking into a squat with your back flat and your knees bent gently. Push your butt out, and rock side to side to really loosen up those thighs. Next, stand up straight in a neutral position, and do a quad stretch by lifting your right leg with your right hand and pulling it back behind you so your foot touches your butt. Hold for 5 seconds, then release and repeat with the other leg.

4. **The arms:** Simply stretch your arms out to the side and held slightly upright, as far as they can go, so that you resemble a starfish. Then lower them back down to neutral and focus on your shoulders. Roll your shoulders to get your blood and circulation flowing. Roll five times to the front, then five times to the back. Alternate the direction for a few rounds.

So take a few minutes to stretch those limbs and rejuvenate your tired body—and relish that instant blast of energy!

READ A POEM

Poetry can be very meaningful, and reading in general stimulates the mind. It allows the brain to process new and interesting information, so you can freely indulge in your own curiosity. Spending just 5 minutes reading a poem will wake up your body and give you a new appreciation for life. Find a poet whose work you haven't read before, and let your mind wander into his or her style, taking in the novelty of it all. Or pick up something you love and have read before that holds a certain influence in your life—a medley of words that are positive and can instantly bring happiness and fulfillment.

If you do this regularly, you'll start to be more emotionally connected to whatever you're feeling, and you'll have a short reminder of something beautiful and inspirational to look forward to each day.

GET OUTSIDE!

If you're feeling sluggish, just get outdoors! Being outside can have an energizing effect on the body, and the fresh air can rejuvenate your mind and soul. In fact, studies have shown that nature can improve energy levels by introducing oxygenated blood into the body through each breath outdoors. You see, that deep breath of fresh air—thanks to the presence of trees and flowers—brings oxygen into the lungs which then purifies the blood and gives you an energy kick. And it's better than simply breathing indoors—a study published in *The Journal of Environmental Psychology* showed that being in nature energized 90 percent of participants! And as little as 5 minutes outside in a park or running a trip to the drugstore can instantly give you that much-needed boost. You can take these 5-minute breaks a few times each day to maximize the energizing benefits and have steadier energy stores throughout the day.

In addition, nature has also been proven to spark creativity and productivity, so you'll feel invigorated at work and at home with the people you love. You'll be better able to think outside the box and tackle exciting and innovative projects. There are so many ways to get in touch with nature, so carving out 5 minutes at least once a day shouldn't be too difficult. Here are some ideas.

Get Some Fresh Air

1. Take a brisk 5-minute walk in the park. Here you'll find beautiful trees, flowers, and probably some ants. The beauty will help you reset and feel more focused and energized.
2. Grab a bike and hit the trails. If you're in a city, use a bike-sharing service and go for a ride. Let the breeze wash over you.
3. Stop and smell the roses. If you're near a park, pond, or garden, you can take a moment and smell the flowers. If you're in a busier city and can't find immediate access, stop inside a flower shop for 5 minutes and let the plants renew you.
4. Awaken your senses by smelling something that reminds you of nature, even if you can't make it outside. For instance, you can buy a candle for your desk or carry essential oils to smell the ocean, grass, or a campfire. All of these aromas will improve energy levels and fight stress.

Take that short break outdoors to awaken your mind and body. You're sure to feel a great energy boost that can last for hours once you return inside.

MEDITATE!

Meditation is an art that takes time and dedication to learn, but once you've honed those skills, the benefits will make it worthwhile. It's a way to connect with your thoughts and focus your mind, so once the meditation is over, you'll feel energized and eager to tackle whatever's next on your to-do list. Research has shown that meditation can alleviate symptoms of depression and fight anxiety, bettering your quality of life and overall well-being. It also sharpens your brain and memory retention, thereby lowering the risk of dementia and Alzheimer's disease.

Meditation is a spiritual practice, and if you make a commitment to do it each day for 5 minutes, you'll become more in tune with your emotions, thoughts, worries, and desires. You can meditate in silence or listen to a guided meditation to help you get the hang of it. Starting your practice with background noise or soothing sounds might make for an easier adjustment to the art of meditation, and it may even help you focus better.

If you're not sure how to get started, here are some tips:

- Start small, with only 5 minutes at a time each day, and choose a quiet area to be free of distractions. You can also set a soft alarm to give yourself 5 minutes and forego checking the clock.
- Sit on a chair or put a pillow underneath your butt for a cushion so you can be comfortable. When sitting, keep your back

straight with good posture, and either open or close your eyes, depending on your personal preference.

- Look slightly downward, focusing your attention on the ground in front of you.
- Then be still and silent, letting energy and power course through your veins.

After you do this for 5 minutes, you'll feel refreshed and awake.

MAKE A DREAM LIST

If you consider yourself a dreamer, you're one step closer to finding more vigor and enthusiasm for life and its greatest gifts. Have you wanted to go skydiving? Climb to the top of a mountain? Visit Europe? Run a marathon? These are all dreams that can absolutely come true, as long as you believe in their power and make moves that can lead up to these accomplishments. Reminding yourself of these dreams, and taking 5 minutes a day to add a few more or cross some off your list, will keep you energized and full of the motivation you need to go after the things you want in life. You get only one life, and every second is precious—so make the most out of each one!

To make a dream list, do the following:

1. Write down a dream you have.
2. Jot down three to four sentences describing what the dream entails, why you want it, how you will feel once you've accomplished it, and how it ranks in terms of priority.
3. When you've accomplished a dream, write a sentence describing what it really felt like and check it off your list.
4. On to the next one!

Both dreaming and acknowledging accomplishments provide stimulation, creating excitement for life's greatest gifts and experiences. Give it a try and enjoy!

TIDY UP!

I'm not saying you have to clean your whole house at once, but taking 5 minutes to tidy up something in your vicinity will provide a burst of energy (you are moving around with a broom or sponge in hand), and it'll help you feel more organized. Studies have shown that being more organized can encourage productivity and alertness, so tidying up could be just the fix for maintaining your stamina during a busy day. Some 5-minute cleanup ideas include the following:

- Put on a favorite song or two to fill the 5-minute span, and get to work on the kitchen. Clean the counters and stove, wiping away any crusty areas or stickiness that might be there from cooking. Organize the fridge and pantry if you have extra time.
- Put your clothes away! I'm sure you've had a night or two where you were too tired to hang up a shirt and ended up placing it on the bedroom chair instead. Clean up your mess, and hang garments in the closet. If you don't have scattered clothes around, simply tackle your closet or drawers by refolding items or color-coordinating a few shirts.
- Make your bathroom tidier. Hairs in the shower? Makeup stains on the countertop? Toothpaste in the sink? See where there's room for improvement, then quickly freshen up the bathroom and get rid of grooming residue.

- Clean dust off the windows. There are so many hidden areas that can get dusty, and we often forget to take care of those places on a regular basis. Fight the buildup by spending 5 minutes to freshen up.
- Vacuum a room. Pick one place in your home and get rid of those dust bunnies. You'll instantly feel cleaner, and the air will just *feel* more invigorating to breathe in.

It's worth noting, however, that research has also suggested that a bit of messiness can spark creativity. Think about it this way: your environment, whether clean or disorderly, will influence how you live your life. Of course, it's best to be on the organized end for the most part so you'll feel invigorated and stable, but if you're looking to use your imagination for a project that requires you to think outside the norm, a few extra papers on the desk might actually help.

READ THE PAPER

Staying up-to-date on what's happening in the news, pop culture, the arts, and more will consistently give you more energy to power your step and seek to interact with the world at large. Not only will you be better equipped to speak your mind, but you'll also be more interested in playing a part in your world and diving into new experiences, topics, and cultural events.

You can get a subscription in print, right at your doorstep, or just read the news online each day. What's a great time to flip through those pages? Grab a newspaper or log on to the Internet early in the morning, along with a cup of java. Starting each day with the news will allow you to indulge your curiosity and boost those brain cells to fuel you for the day ahead. Check out whatever section piques your interest, or look to a few different columns to give you some well-rounded knowledge and diversity. Then, when you meet a friend for lunch or head into the office, you can share what you've just learned to keep that mental stimulation going even longer!

PRACTICE A NEW HOBBY

Have you wanted to learn to sew? Make a chocolate soufflé? Play the piano? Become fluent in a foreign language? Try stand-up comedy or improv? Well, it's not too late—you can pick up one of these hobbies to give your life another energizing purpose.

As long as you practice your new skill for 5 minutes each day, you will make progress over time, and pretty soon you'll be showing off your new talent to those around you! It might seem scary to try something new—especially when you might be pretty bad at it to start—but as long as you stay committed and enthusiastic, you'll naturally improve.

Still, no matter how masterful you become, each time you practice your new hobby, your energy and mood will benefit. Studies show that doing something you're passionate about can drastically enhance well-being and drive. Use your new hobby as something to look forward to after a long day at work or as soon as you open your eyes in the morning. Learning a new hobby is a great way to help you feel connected to the world in those unusual, personal ways that make you who you are!

SING LOUD AND PROUD

Don't let anything stop you from belting out your favorite show tune or doing a fab rendition of an 1980s classic. No matter the audience—be it the patrons of a karaoke bar, a group of close friends and family, your dog, or your showerhead—sing for yourself and let the lyrics energize your soul.

And if you have children, include them in the fun! Kids love singing (though you may need to pick one of today's hits!), and it's a good way to encourage them to get involved in the arts at a young age. Studies have shown that art and music can foster creativity, which will benefit your children as they get older.

As for you? It's enjoyable to let yourself go and be in the moment, and whatever song you choose to sing will certainly hold some meaning for you. Let the words and sentiments take you somewhere else—to a place where you feel alive and free. When you're in need of some liberation during the day, *sing*. Just be mindful of your surroundings, since your location will dictate the volume of your voice.

COMPLIMENT YOURSELF!

Everyone deserves a little praise—*especially* you! While it feels great to receive compliments from others, it's equally important (if not more so) to show yourself some love, acceptance, and appreciation every day. In as little as 5 minutes, you can instantly boost your energy levels—and your mood—by simply saying something you love about yourself or complimenting an attribute, a recent success, or even something as minor as your outfit. It'll boost your ego and confidence so you'll feel eager to attack the day with composure and authority.

We are often hard on ourselves, and it's a shame because no matter our mishaps and failures, we do so many wonderful, honorable things that should be recognized. And for others to find goodness in us, we need to find it in ourselves first. So look at yourself in the mirror and say something you're *dying* to hear, like one of the following:

- Got a new client? Say how proud you are of yourself.
- Reached a new goal in a workout? Tell yourself you're a superstar—lean and courageous.
- Got up the nerve to speak to someone you've had your eye on? Know that doing so took some serious guts.
- Settled a dispute that has been weighing on your shoulders? Breathe a sigh of relief and know you fixed your problem perfectly.

- Made a new friend and expanded your social network? Feel excited about the newfound connection and the experiences you can share together in the future.
- Tried a new food or drink you've been curious about? Be proud of stepping outside your comfort zone.
- Made a difference in someone's life today? Perhaps you donated to a charity, or you made someone laugh? Compliment yourself for your generosity and kindness.

Do whatever's in your heart in the moment, and use that energy boost to get through the rest of the day!

DONATE TO A CHARITY

Donating to better the lives of others and providing care and gratitude will instantly improve your energy levels and make you feel accomplished, proud, and significant. So take 5 minutes to find a charity that piques your interest and decide on an amount of money that's within your means to donate! You don't need to spend too much—do whatever you can afford or feels right for you in that moment.

And you don't even really need to spend money at all—you can also donate your time and effort. Maybe you can donate food items to a food pantry or clothes to a shelter. Donate to a cause that's meaningful and find a way to be there—no financial pressure necessary. It's more about the thoughts and actions themselves in influencing energy levels. Plus, you can do this each day, if you choose, as a way to give back and feel energized regularly. Those small donations will surely add up into a very generous one.

EAT WHOLE GRAINS

Refined grains, like those found in baked goods and white bread, can zap your energy and slow your metabolism. But whole grains are rich in B vitamins, complex carbohydrates, and fiber—all of which work together to keep you full and maintain steady energy stores. What's the difference between whole grains versus refined grains, such as white rice? Whole grains, like quinoa and brown rice, contain fiber and key nutrients to keep you full, and they encourage the body to digest them slowly, leaving you with more energy for a longer period of time.

What's more, refined grains are higher on the glycemic index, meaning they can spike blood sugar, especially when paired with sweets (think of a blueberry muffin). Whole grains are much lower on the scale, so you can avoid that surge and subsequent crash in energy later—which defeats the whole purpose of that instant jolt, right? Pair grains with extra protein and healthy fats for a well-rounded meal or snack.

Whole Grains to Consider

- Amaranth
- Barley
- Brown rice
- Buckwheat
- Bulgur
- Quinoa

- Rye
- Sorghum
- Spelt
- Wheat

Eating a serving of these whole grains, along with some protein and good fats, will create stable energy levels to tide you over until your next meal. And they're delicious as well!

EMBRACE THE WATER

There's something very calming and awakening about the water, whether it be a pool, the beach, or even your shower. When you think about it, it makes sense—people often take showers in the morning to wipe the sleep off their dreary eyelids and get themselves out the door. Water can signify birth and renewal, a clean slate, and a way to wash away any fears, worries, or toxins standing in your way. It can clear the body and mind and create balance, a flow of energy, and restoration.

If you live near a pool or beach, find time to hit the waves! Go surfing or swimming, or just dip your toes into the water. If you don't have easy access to a pool or beach, find a pool at a nearby gym, draw a bath, or take a shower. Give yourself 5 minutes to really be with the water and with your thoughts—let the water uplift and energize your mind and body.

STAY HYDRATED!

It's not enough to just bathe in H_2O—your body is about 60 percent water so when you become dehydrated, your energy levels can drop. Plus, if you become dehydrated, you could be in trouble—severe dehydration can lead to faintness, lightheadedness, nausea, muscle cramps, and more.

Simply put, water is life—it's life's energy source—and your body needs it desperately. By drinking enough fluid throughout the day, you will keep your body in balance, improving organ function and keeping your mood and energy levels stable. Take 5 minutes to drink one glass, then repeat this activity a few times during the day. Aim for at least eight glasses of water a day, and increase this number if you're prone to heavy sweating or highly active. If you don't like the taste of plain water, don't worry—turn basic water into a fruity sensation by adding fresh fruits along with herbs, such as mint or rosemary, to a pitcher in the fridge.

GET COOKING!

You've probably heard the phrase "You are what you eat." Well, it's true! While you might be crunched for time or really like your Chinese takeout, cooking a healthy meal at home can be great for both your short- and long-term energy levels. Why? Well, in the privacy of your own kitchen, you can make the process lively and stimulating simply by putting on your favorite playlist or watching a TV show while chopping vegetables or preheating the stove. (Although there's nothing wrong with some tasty Chinese takeout every now and then.)

Make it a priority to break out your pots and pans and whip up a nutritious, flavorful meal for the whole family to enjoy. Beyond the energizing benefits of cooking itself, the enjoyment you know your family will have when they taste your meal will provide an even greater boost. Besides, not only will cooking provide reassurance that what you're eating is good for you, but it'll also prevent a big dent in your wallet. When you think about it, those restaurant meals and takeout orders can surely add up.

You can even cook meals in bulk, such as grains and vegetables or a whole roasted chicken at once, and then use the leftovers during the week. Simply heat them up, and they'll ready in 5 minutes. The accomplishment of getting a few meals out of the way will make you feel more energized and eager for the remainder of the week.

HAVE MEALTIME WITH FAMILY

No matter how big or small, unconventional or traditional, family is family, and it should be prioritized, especially when it comes to mealtime. Studies show that whether you're sitting down together for breakfast, lunch, or dinner, the act of breaking bread and sharing stimulating conversations with those you love can boost your energy levels and may make you feel grateful for the life that you're living together. And a renewed zest for life and a sense of gratitude aren't the only things that you gain from family dinner!

If you have children, research has shown that dinnertime as a family can improve children's intelligence and well-being, helping them grow to be strong, independent adults with a good head on their shoulders. Plus, you'll benefit too! Having a close network and socializing regularly enhances quality of life, so you'll feel happier each day knowing that you'll all be reunited at the dinner table. When you're together, make a plan to bond as a family—which means the TV should *probably* be turned off unless it's movie night or a big game is on. That said, every family dynamic is different, so do whatever feels right!

GET RID OF TOXIC ELEMENTS

In life, there are so many things that can drain your energy. Consider toxic friendships, bad lifestyle habits, germs and uncleanliness, and more. It's important to check in to see what aspects are contributing energy and fruition to your life and which aspects need to be kicked to the curb.

Make a list and evaluate. For those relationships and habits that are toxic, it will be hard to separate from them at first, especially if they have become deep-rooted habits or they involve relatively close relationships with a lot of history, but the cut will be beneficial in the end.

Get Rid of Toxins

1. **Remove yourself from negative relationships.** Do you have a friend who always seems to disappoint you or get you into trouble? A bad influence, when it comes to your behaviors and your feelings, can be troublesome and zap you of energy and happiness. It will be hard to break the connection, but with time you'll heal.
2. **Quit smoking.** Smoking isn't good for your health, as it increases the risk of various diseases and death. There's nothing invigorating about that! It's definitely challenging to break a habit, but strive to get help so you no longer need a cigarette for "immediate" energy. You'll have much more "long-term" energy for the rest of your life.
3. **Clean your home.** Living in dirty conditions can make you tired and sick, which will only get worse the longer you let things go. Make

a point to keep your home clean—that means regularly washing dishes, cleaning countertops, changing the bedsheets, and wiping away dust. A solution? You can make more of an effort to clean up your space—see some suggestions in "Tidy Up!" in Part 1—or you can make a quick call and hire a cleaning person to come and take care of it.

BE OPEN TO LOVE

It can be hard to let love in—there's a natural fear in people when it comes to getting close to someone new, being vulnerable, and accepting that things might not work out, at which point the heart will need time to recover and bounce back. However, if you can put those anxieties aside and be open to affection and warmth, the rewards will bring a remarkable flow of vigor and strength that'll flow through your body—especially your heart!

Love comes in many forms: love from yourself, family, friends, a significant other, and even a pet. Love can also be associated with a passion—such as music, film, or sports. Figure out the areas where you need more love in your life, and work toward making connections that can fill that void. Devote 5 minutes each day to engage in this love, and build on it. Here are some ideas:

- Give someone you love a quick embrace. If it's a partner, give a kiss on the lips, cheek, or forehead. If it's a friend, a hug or a pat on the back might be better.
- Take 5 minutes to play with your pet or to watch a cute video of a pet online.
- Spend a few moments to enjoy a tasty snack—something you love that will make you feel energized and happy.
- Love to sing or dance? Turn on some music or just belt out a tune and break out some dance moves.

- Videochat with a relative or friend living in another city for a quick catch-up.
- Spontaneously ask your partner for a "date night" to deepen your relationship.
- Doodle a few symbols of love, such as a heart or lips. The images will make you feel more open to love.
- Look at a photo of a moment where you were in love, whether it's with a hobby or a person.
- Write down three things you love about the world and three things you'd like to fall in love with in the future.
- Give your body a quick massage—show yourself some love!

And once you do find love, hold on to it. Let it work its powers and bring meaning and hope to your life so every moment is truly special.

EAT MINDFULLY

There's an art when it comes to mindfulness, especially in terms of eating. Many people rush through every meal they eat, thanks to the increasingly popular diet of fast food and large portion sizes. We end up polishing off our meals in a matter of minutes. But rushing through a meal doesn't allow your mind and body to absorb the energy and nutrients you are taking in, and it can lead to poor digestion, which will lower energy levels and provide discomfort later on. This bad habit can cause people to overeat or feel hungry later because we're not giving our bodies time to register fullness, and we're often eating high-carb, high-fat foods that are loaded with sugar and don't provide long-lasting energy. In fact, we're then more likely to crash later, feeling even more lethargic from the quickly digested meal. The solution? Take 5 minutes to reflect on the taste and experience and let that energy circulate throughout your body, hitting all your senses. What are you eating? How is it making you feel? Taking the time to check in and enjoy yourself will give you a whole new outlook toward dining. It will make the experience of digging into your tender filet mignon more magical and memorable, and you'll feel a hit of energy with each bite and swallow.

1. Take a small bite and chew, putting the fork down.
2. Let the food melt in your mouth as you take slow bites. Be sure to take at least five to ten bites.

3. Wait a minute before taking another bite to start to register fullness. Check in with how your body and stomach are feeling; look to your appetite for clues.
4. Repeat this process.

DITCH THE SUGAR

Sugar will drain your energy—even if you notice an immediate spike in your energy level, you'll likely experience the subsequent crash once the sugar's effect has worn off. Sugar can also increase inflammation in the body, leading to higher risk of diseases such as diabetes, heart disease, and cancer. That inflammation will also hurt your brain, causing you to lose focus and clarity.

Sugar shouldn't be off-limits, as it's nice to indulge on occasion and natural sugar, such as those found in fruit, does offer benefits. But it's all about moderation. So the next time you want to grab a sugar-filled food or drink, take 5 minutes to consider the sugar and opt for a healthier swap. Some examples of more energizing sources of food are given in the following list:

High-Sugar Foods and Low-Sugar Substitutes

- **Soda:** Swap in unsweetened tea or lightly flavored water instead.
- **Baked goods:** Try indulging in a square or two of dark chocolate instead.
- **High-sugar and fattening condiments:** These include ketchup, mayonnaise, and barbecue sauces. Try using low-sodium sauces, such as soy sauce, or healthy oils, such as olive oil and avocado oil instead.
- **Candy:** It's no surprise to find candy on this list! If you're craving candy give naturally sweet fruit, such as a fresh apple or a cup of berries with whipped cream (for a light dip) a try.

- **Juices:** Commonly considered healthy, juice is packed with sugar! Instead quench your thirst with water infused with fruit slices or sparkling zero-calorie water, like Zevia.
- **Dried fruit:** You'll find foods like raisins, cranberries, banana chips, and mango in this category. Swap them out for fresh fruit, such as melon, a banana, an apple, or a pear!

EAT ENOUGH IRON

Iron is super important for keeping your energy levels up. It plays a major role in bodily function and red blood cell production. Red blood cells carry hemoglobin, an iron-rich protein, throughout the body to improve absorption and digestion of key vitamins and minerals and to improve the circulation of fresh, oxygenated blood. That's why many people who are anemic, meaning they are deficient in iron, experience fatigue and lack of focus.

If you don't think you're getting enough iron (about 18 milligrams of iron a day for a healthy adult), you should try to get your fill from whole foods, including lean proteins like beef, chicken, and fish, beans and legumes, and leafy greens. However, if you're still not able to get enough, you might want to supplement. Of course, speak to a doctor first before taking any pills. Work toward integrating more iron-packed foods into your meals and snacks, though, as that's the best way to reap those energizing benefits of iron.

Top Iron Sources Based on Milligrams per Serving

- Red meat (2.7 milligrams per 4-ounce serving)
- Chicken (1.2 milligrams per 4-ounce serving)
- Fish (0.4 milligrams per 4-ounce serving)
- Beans and legumes (1.8 milligrams per ½-cup serving)
- Spinach (3.2 milligrams per ½-cup serving)

- Tofu (1.2 milligrams per 4-ounce serving)
- Shrimp (3.6 milligrams per 4-ounce serving)
- Pumpkin seeds (4.2 milligrams per 1-ounce serving)
- Dried apricots (0.7 milligrams per 1-ounce serving)

Try pairing beans, greens, and meat together for a well-rounded, iron-rich meal. Or snack on roasted chickpeas and seeds for a snack in the afternoon. Whatever high-iron food you choose, you're sure to get the energy boost that follows!

DON'T SWEAT THE SMALL STUFF

If you freak out over every setback or worry, you'll start to feel drained, and it'll be hard to break out of that negative mood. While there are certain things in life that are worth fretting about—losing your job, moving to a new city, or missing an important event—smaller, more trivial obstacles shouldn't hold too much weight, so don't let them drive you crazy! Instead, take 5 minutes to acknowledge that a minor mistake is okay—you will overcome it.

Consider who it affected, what the actual *worst* outcome could be, and what you really think is going to happen before you get too unsettled. Also, think rationally—is there a way you can fix the problem? How can you make up for the mistake? By thinking with a sense of calm and having a determined attitude, you'll feel energized and empowered to stand strong and make things right, rather than getting too caught up in the worries and negativity of it all.

TAKE A PROBIOTIC

Pour a glass of water and take a probiotic supplement each day to keep your gut healthy and your energy up. Studies have shown that there are many benefits of probiotics, which are microorganisms that act on the digestive process and gut. They include the following:

- Promoting better digestive health and immunity
- Increasing the amount of good bacteria in the gut
- Decreasing strains of bad bacteria in the gut
- Stimulating regular bowel movements

Studies have shown that probiotics' effects on the immune system and digestion can improve energy levels and fight chronic fatigue. By feeling healthier overall and having better digestion, you're less likely to feel sluggish. Beyond taking a supplement, which you can find at any drugstore, you can also eat probiotic-rich foods. These include the following:

- Sauerkraut
- Miso
- Sourdough bread
- Kimchi
- Greek yogurt (not regular)
- Kefir

- Kombucha (see the "Sip Kombucha!" entry in Part 3)
- And more!

Try adding these probiotic-packed foods to your dishes as seasonings or sauces to boost flavor and nutrition. You can also ferment foods yourself, like peppers, carrots, and artichokes. Simply place them in a mason jar, add a little salt, and fill with water for brining, then move the jar to cold storage. Look for a few signs to know it's ready: there should be bubbling, a sour smell, and a tangy flavor.

DON'T FORGET ABOUT PREBIOTICS

Probiotics are great energy boosters! (Just see the "Take a Probiotic" entry earlier in this part.) But you can't eat probiotics alone for the full energy-boosting benefits—you need to try prebiotics as well! Prebiotics are the guys that feed the probiotics, allowing them to work their magic on your gut. Eating a healthy diet that's high in both prebiotics and probiotics is your best bet at maintaining smooth digestion and stable energy levels. After all, when your belly hurts or you experience cramps and bloating after a meal, your energy levels can plummet instantly. However, by being mindful of prebiotic and probiotic intake in tandem, you'll have a greater supply of energy to stay alert throughout the day. Where can you find prebiotics? A few prebiotic sources include the following:

- Bananas
- Asparagus
- Garlic
- Onion
- Leeks
- Jerusalem artichokes
- And more!

To make getting both probiotics *and* prebiotics into your diet more easily, consider where you can combine both types of microorganisms into your meals. For instance:

- Chop a banana into slices for a Greek yogurt parfait or kefir smoothie
- Use miso dressing for a garnish on grilled or sautéed asparagus with garlic and onion
- Chop some garlic into balsamic vinegar and spread on sourdough toast for a savory dip

Take a few minutes to come up with recipes that feature both prebiotics and probiotics. It'll make meal planning a snap—and your energy levels are sure to benefit in a big way!

CHANNEL YOUR INNER YOGI

Yoga has long been touted for its benefits in improving the mind and body connection, and it's a powerful energizer that can be practiced anywhere. Simply taking 5 minutes to do a series of poses will restore your drained energy and provide mental stimulation. While you'll find entries in the other parts of the book that offer info on how a number of yoga poses can boost your energy levels, performing a *yoga flow*, where you go through a series of a few poses at once, can provide a major energy boost. The movement from one pose to the next provides a rhythm that will awaken the limbs to enhance flexibility and mobility as well as enhance circulation and blood flow, providing a fresh source of vitality. Opening the body and flowing through a sequence of motions uses consistent movement to free pent-up tension, which will get you moving even more once those 5 minutes are over.

What's more, a regular yoga practice has been shown to lower stress and anxiety levels, so you'll feel calmer and more in control of your life overall. This ease will make you happier and motivated, so you'll be more eager to live life to its fullest potential. Plus, if you face challenges—which are inevitable, of course—this sense of control and the ability to calm and center yourself will come in handy, helping you fight through the obstacles and find a favorable outcome.

Energy-Boosting Poses to Try

- **Locust Pose:** To try this pose, lie facedown on the floor, then lift your legs, arms, chest, and head off the floor until you're resting solely on your stomach.
- **Standing Forward Bend:** To try this pose, keep your legs straight and bend down slowly toward the floor. Let your head hang down, facing the ground, and reach your palms to the floor. Hold, then come up to standing.
- **Pigeon Pose:** To try this pose, sit on the ground with the knee of your front leg out to the side with your leg bent. Stretch your back leg out behind you. Sink into the ground to open up those hips. Rest your hands in front of you, close to the ground, for a deeper stretch. Repeat, switching legs.
- **Bridge Pose:** To try this pose, lie down with your back on the floor, bend your knees, and set your feet flat on the floor, with your heels as close to your sitting bones as possible. Lift your buttocks up off the floor and hold.
- **Garland Pose:** To try this pose, stand with your feet as close together as possible, and sink down into a squat with your elbows pressed against your inner knees. Clasp your palms together, keep your back straight, and hold the pose.

Practice these poses in a 5-minute sequence, and when you finally get through a whole set, you'll be energized and ready to take on the world!

CONSIDER A "WHAT IF" SCENARIO

It can be hard to reflect on what could happen if it doesn't seem as though the opportunity is realistic or somewhere in the near future. But unfortunately, when you don't take the time to think about what *could* happen if you take a leap and spark change, you run the risk of staying stagnant and losing your shot. Stagnation drains energy—it leaves you stuck, unable to move forward.

So it's okay to daydream and think about something positive that could happen—in fact, it's encouraged! Not only does daydreaming improve your mood and create feelings of excitement and hope, but it also helps you get in tune with your desires, goals, and thoughts—and this gives you the energy you need to make those dreams a reality! To have a steady zest for life, try the following activities:

1. Write down three "what if" scenarios on a piece of paper. For example, consider:
   - "What if" you were to ask your boss if you could work from home on Fridays? Would that give you more flexibility to be with your family? More opportunity for travel? How would that create more energy in your life?
   - "What if" you were to join a new gym or book club you've had your eye on? Would the health kick make you more eager to tackle the day? Would you feel energized from the workouts?

Would the book club broaden your friendships and bring more excitement to your social life?

- "What if" you were to move to a city you've always dreamed of living in? Would you feel energized and happier each morning? Would you feel more accustomed to the weather or culture there? Would it create better career advancements or a community for your family?

2. Close your eyes and envision your "what ifs." Let yourself enjoy the full experience, and create a story for yourself in your head. Let the sounds, sights, smells, and more come to life.
3. Smile—then figure out how to turn that "what if" into a reality.

Keep that forward momentum going, and you can achieve all your dreams and start to come up with new "what ifs"!

TOUCH SOMEONE GENTLY

Human contact is critical for happiness and fulfillment—it brings you closer to those around you and activates hormones, such as oxytocin, that can enhance mood and energy levels. The mere act of touching another human reminds you of the power of intimacy and how we as humans long for it in order to feel purposeful, accepted, and loved. These emotions will drive you to commit—to people, to activities you love, to work, to *everything*. This vigor, and the energy boost that accompanies it, can push you to make the most of your life, since you'll be so grateful for all that you've already been given.

So take 5 minutes to touch someone! How?

- Hug or kiss a friend on the cheek.
- Kiss your partner on the lips and utter, "I love you."
- Make time for sex.
- Congratulate a friend on an accomplishment with a pat on the back.

No matter what it is, find a way to connect physically.

TAKE A PHOTO OF YOUR PET

Nothing can give you that immediate surge in energy as much as your pet can. Let's be honest; your pet (no matter what kind you have) is a true friend who is always upbeat, playful, and there for you in your time of need. So take out your phone's camera and snap a photo of the two of you together! You can snuggle on the sofa, take a selfie in a dog park, or record a video of the two of you playing catch. Take a moment to study your pet's face: looking at the eyes, smile, and little changes in fur shade or marks on the skin. Realize how much you love every spot and trait you see—how this unconditional best friend is yours, always there to lend an energizing smile and warm nature.

Capture a few beautiful moments with your furry best friend to feel more energized and supported. You should save the image on your phone so you can access it whenever you feel tired or bitter and need a reminder of how lucky you are to have your pet in your life.

LOOK FOR CLOUD ART!

Step outside and look up at a cloud. Can you see an image? A cat? A flower? A clown? A person drinking a cup of coffee? Well, the last one is probably unlikely, but this activity is all about using creativity and imagination to improve your energy levels. And not only is this activity mentally stimulating—since it forces you to use your brain and really focus on finding something new and unconventional in an unexpected place—but it also gets you outside, where the fresh air can awaken you.

Studies link creativity to a higher quality of life and cognitive function, which means that this 5-minute activity's benefits will carry over as you head back inside. So take a look and find an image in just one cloud, or feel free to pick a few! Your energy levels will thank you!

POUR A GLASS OF WINE

Yes, you can have that glass of wine! Red wine is high in antioxidants that can improve skin, heart, and brain health. One of these antioxidants is resveratrol, which fights aging and free radical damage (a type of toxicity amongst other oxidants), in the body, which can lead to inflammation and a higher risk of disease. Inflammation can lead to fatigue, a weakened immune system, and higher stress levels, all of which can zap energy stores. So by keeping inflammation at bay, you'll have more stable energy and stamina to get through the day!

Red wine can fight stress, relieving any tension that could be draining you—and that is also an energy boost. There's no need to drink daily, but drinking one glass a day for women or two for men is perfectly fine for most healthy adults. In fact, studies have found that drinking alcohol in moderation can improve well-being and health, especially when it comes to red wine! However, going overboard can backfire, so resist an extra heavy pour. Drinking too much wine can make you drowsy and alcohol is a depressant, meaning it can make you excessively tired, which all leads to plummeting energy levels. So feel free to enjoy that glass of wine, but keep an eye on how much you're taking in.

FORGIVE YOURSELF

The simplest way to have a sunnier spring in your step is to just cut yourself some slack. As humans, we are often our own worst critics—and when we mess up or do something we disapprove of, it's hard to let it go and forgive ourselves for the harm we've caused. However, feeling negative and guilty will cause a dramatic and instantaneous drop in your energy levels and your self-confidence! So use the power of 5-minute forgiveness in two ways to boost your energy and spark happiness:

1. If you're feeling guilty and beating yourself up at the time of the incident, it's okay to feel bad—acknowledge it. However, move on from there to lift your energy. Use these 5 minutes to accept and forgive. Use your mistake as a learning step so you can avoid making the same mistake in the future, and let it pass. Look ahead, and feel energized about being better in the future.
2. If you're in need of a quick energy lift, it's time to let go of something you did in the past but never came to terms with. Forgive yourself for an argument, a missed work deadline, or even something as simple as forgetting to hold the door open for someone.

By freeing yourself of the weight on your shoulders, you'll feel lighter on your feet with more energy and glee.

INDULGE!

Life is about balance—and that means you should be able to energize yourself by indulging in something special every day. Make it small—a video clip that makes you laugh, a few spritzes of perfume, a bite or two of your favorite food—then change it up and relish in the moments. Yes, that means you can and *should* make room for desserts and salty snacks. In fact, when it comes to dieting, having an 80/20 lifestyle, where you eat clean for 80 percent of the time and enjoy sweets and "less healthy" foods for 20 percent, has been shown to provide the greatest benefits and staying power.

When you restrict yourself from life's pleasures, you run the risk of burnout, where you might act out in the opposite manner and sabotage your positive intentions. This vicious cycle zaps energy and may increase feelings of depression, anxiety, and resentment. So make it a point to take 5 minutes each day to do something just for *you*! Try anything that makes you feel special, alive, and not deprived one bit!

PART 2
ENERGIZE YOUR MIND

THINK POSITIVELY!

Studies have shown how positive thinking can work to improve energy levels, cognitive function, memory retention, and overall happiness. When the mind is weighed down with negativity and anxiety, that stress can affect the body all over—causing brain cells to rupture, increased inflammation, and chronic fatigue. When we are too caught up in negativity, we lose motivation, which can make us feel sluggish, insecure, and more prone to succumbing to defeat. What's more, all of these factors put you at greater risk of disease and death. However, spending just 5 minutes a day engaging in intentional positive thinking can keep your brain sharp and troubles at bay, giving you a more energized outlook on life and its greatest pleasures. Here's an activity that will declutter your mind and free it from negative thoughts:

1. Think about what's troubling you. What thoughts and feelings are on your mind? What is causing you stress?
2. Close your eyes, and imagine these thoughts and words being swept away by the ocean. Let the waves take them away, somewhere far off in the distance.
3. Breathe in through your nose and out through your mouth. Take this moment to feel relief. Let out a sigh. Look forward to a fresh start. Open your eyes with newfound energy.

By taking a few moments to feel positivity abound, you'll feel invigorated to spark change and improve your quality of life.

TAKE AN ONLINE QUIZ

You know those trivia or personality quizzes you can find online? Take 5 minutes to test your knowledge, learn more about yourself, and boost your energy levels!

If you take a personality quiz where you answer questions that apply to your character, you'll discover more about your true self, which can create instant energy and make you feel more alive in the world. Now, I don't mean those fluffy, entertaining quizzes like "Which TV Character Are You?"! I'm talking about quizzes that reveal deep truths or provide insight into your character. These quizzes might be assessing your dominant traits, looking at your love languages, determining your sleep style and what that means for your personality and core set of values, etc. When you understand yourself better and are more in tune with your thoughts, behaviors, and desires, you're more apt to go after your goals with newfound empowerment and stride. The sense of belonging and self-recognition is a powerful motivator for positive change and action.

If you opt for trivia or a more academic quiz like mathematical word problems, you might not learn much about yourself, but you'll still activate the mind and get those energetic juices flowing. When you set your mind to a challenge, you are boosting alertness and using problem-solving methods to wake yourself up. Studies have also shown that regularly expanding and testing the mind through trivia and problem-solving activity can lower the risk of dementia and Alzheimer's disease as well as improve cognitive abilities in those suffering.

So bookmark a few of your favorite websites for easy access, and get those energy levels soaring!

TRY MINDFULNESS MEDITATION

As you learned in the "Meditate!" entry in Part 1, meditation centers the mind and frees it from negative or excessive thoughts. It's a great way to become more aware of your surroundings and the present moment without letting life's hectic nature seize your brain. No matter your whereabouts, you can spare 5 minutes to engage in a mindful meditation, which can be in silence or through a guided resource.

What's the difference between mindfulness meditation and standard meditation? Mindfulness meditation requires you to focus on a single object, which might be a vase in the center of the room, a gong that's rhythmically beating, or your breath. It uses a focal point or source to channel that meditative energy and bring about a centered awareness to the present moment.

Each time you do a mindful meditation, you are strengthening your brain cells, boosting cognitive function, and building awareness and energy. It will take time, so don't get defeated, especially when those pervading thoughts about what to make for dinner that night or how you need to RSVP to a friend's event later in the week appear during your meditation time. It's a skill that requires practice, so if you find yourself struggling through the meditation or you feel bored, give it a few more chances to really provide those mental benefits. Here's what to do, where you're focusing on the breath as your mark and you'll work your body, breath, and thoughts in one:

1. Sit either on the floor with your legs crossed or in a chair.
2. Close your eyes, and keep your limbs and thoughts still.
3. Breathe in and out. Inhale and exhale. Alternate slowly—really getting the full expansion of breath. Focus on the breath alone, clearing your mind of all thoughts.
4. If a thought arises (Need to do laundry later? What to make for dinner? You feel cold in the space you're in?), acknowledge the thought as an observer. Let it stay with you and then leave. Go back to the breath.
5. Repeat this pattern for 5 minutes.

You can also find guided mindfulness meditations online or on an app for your phone. Feel free to put on meditation sounds if you don't want the guided presence but need some background noise. The noises may vary based on the app you decide to use, but they might resemble nature sounds, such as waves crashing or birds chirping. Aim to practice mindfulness meditation once a day to start, but if you're able to work up to a few times each day, you'll really start to learn how to keep the mind energized and in control.

SOLVE A PUZZLE!

No assistance allowed here. Putting those brain cells to work on a puzzle, such as a sudoku, a crossword, or even an old-school cardboard jigsaw puzzle, will stimulate your mind and give you an immediate boost in energy! You can find these puzzles anywhere—a bookstore, an airport, a toy store, or online. Set aside 5 minutes to do one. Even if you can't finish it in time, you can always get back to it later. You'll still get that energy boost even if you don't finish since you're forcing your brain to work aggressively in a short amount of time.

With practice you'll start to get better and better at these sorts of puzzles. You'll find yourself retaining much of the knowledge you've learned and seeing it carry over into other formats. Stash a book of puzzles in your bag so you can always have one on hand for when you're in need of a mental jolt.

LEARN A FEW NEW WORDS!

Gaining knowledge shouldn't end upon finishing school—every day you should be learning something new to keep your mind energized and curious. Continued learning also fosters personal growth and stable energy stores by letting your field of knowledge expand into interesting new territories and subjects that bring excitement and novelty.

Of course, you don't need to learn the entire history of the Incas to feel reenergized! All you need to do is learn five new words each day to energize the mind and keep it sharp for the long term. How can you do this? Grab a dictionary, open it to a random page, close your eyes, and put your finger somewhere on the page. If your finger landed on a word you don't know, learn it! If it's one you already know, just browse the rest of the page and pick out a word you haven't heard of before. Repeat this exercise for 5 minutes, and see how much you can learn in that period of time!

STRIKE UP A CONVERSATION WITH A STRANGER

Conversation, by itself, is stimulating to the mind, but when it comes to one with someone you haven't met before, the novelty of the situation makes it even more interesting. It's the easiest way to get a quick burst of mental energy, as you can find a stranger *anywhere*. Whether you are simply asking for directions or a recommendation for a great place to grab a bite, or whether you stop someone on the street to pay a compliment or inquire where he or she purchased a bag or shirt, it doesn't take much effort, and it'll lead to some sort of light discussion.

Plus, human connection in general has been shown to improve energy and mood, so this type of interaction is a no-brainer when it comes to brain-boosting benefits. If you're shy, start by approaching people you work with or know but haven't spoken to very often. It's a good starting point toward working your way up to meeting a stranger.

CHEW PEPPERMINT GUM

Studies show that the smell of peppermint can uplift mood and energy as well as bring a sense of mental clarity and focus. Plus, the act of chewing can help limit distractions, since it forces your body to stay active and alert. So grab a stick whenever you feel your energy sagging or if your brain starts to feel fatigued.

The effects will be immediate—you'll suddenly feel back on track and eager to tackle whatever's on your plate. This gum hack will surely come in handy during an afternoon slump at work or when you're stuck in traffic during a long commute. Choose a type of gum that is sugar-free, and chew as needed. However, be cautious—excess gum can make you bloated and gassy, so going through a pack a day could be too much.

While gum is easy to keep handy and chewing it will simultaneously give you an energy boost and fresh breath, if you're not a fan of gum, you can always carry peppermint essential oil with you and smell it as needed throughout the day. As long as you have the peppermint factor, your energy levels won't know the difference!

TAKE ON TREE POSE

If you want to feel more energized in your mind, you need it in your body too. That's where yoga comes in. Tree Pose, also known as *Vrksasana*, helps stabilize the body, which in turns brings stability and a flow of energy to the mind. It is also a powerful stretch, offering expansion through the thighs, core, and shoulders, and it strengthens muscles from head to toe. You can do Tree Pose anywhere.

Instructions for Tree Pose

1. Stand straight with your arms at your sides.
2. Shift your body to the left, gently bend your right knee, and slowly lift the right leg off the ground. Reach for your right foot with your right hand.
3. Pull your right foot to your left inner thigh and let it remain there. Your foot can be above or below the knee, depending on flexibility and range of motion.
4. Hold this pose. Clasp your hands in prayer position, with palms held against each other at your chest, then lift them overhead.
5. Pick a point to gaze at in front of you for balance. Hold for a minute. Repeat on the other side. Keep up with this repetition for a total of 5 minutes.

By spending 5 minutes in Tree Pose, you will walk away stimulated and alert.

DOODLE!

Research has shown that doodling can be a form of art, sparking creativity and the imagination and helping you feel more invigorated and productive throughout the day. Carry a notepad with you when you're on the go, so you can head to a local coffee shop and take 5 minutes to draw whatever's on your mind. (And maybe get a cup of coffee while you're there, too!)

Keep notebooks or sticky notes on your desk at the office—it's okay to take the time between work calls to draw freely—or on your kitchen counter at home. Doodling will actually free your mind and give it fresh stimulation to get on with the day. Your doodles don't need to be good— no one's judging your artistic talents here. It's more about letting your mind take off on its own and having that liberation to explore and create. If you're sentimental, feel free to hold on to your doodles! You can buy a notepad dedicated to the doodles themselves, or you can throw them all together in a binder for safekeeping.

RUB YOUR TEMPLES

There's a reason massage therapists work on the temples during a massage. Rubbing the temples alleviates tension in the head, which can affect the entire body and change mood and energy states. The head holds a lot of weight, and when it's fatigued or the mind is burdened by negative thoughts, it drags you down. Applying pressure to the temples stimulates blood flow in the brain and relaxes the forehead, which builds energy and focus and banishes stress.

If you feel tired or stressed out, take a few moments to close your eyes and rub your temples ever so gently. You can even combine the pressure with an essential oil to activate both touch and smell and further boost energy levels.

Some oils in particular have been proven to improve mental stimulation and awareness, such as peppermint, rosemary, basil, sage, lemon, jasmine, cinnamon, and juniper berry. Carry oils with you, or store them in your office and home. As for cinnamon, you can always sprinkle some on food and take a good whiff—try a bowl of oatmeal, Greek yogurt, or a sliced apple. Before using essential oils, speak to your primary physician. There are certain rules regarding essential oil use for those with particular medications and conditions. For examples, you might not be able to use them if you are pregnant or of too young an age.

RECITE POWERFUL WORDS

Pick a few words that evoke power and deeper meaning to you, and say them aloud with volume and authority. Let these words give you energy and confidence when you're losing stamina. Research has shown that thinking about power can in turn make you feel more formidable too. A few suggestions include these:

- Strong
- Bold
- Leadership
- Bravery
- Poise
- Significance
- Resilience

Recite each word five times, but take a deep breath in between each utterance. This will allow your mind to register the word and your body to react. Go through five or so words total. After each word, think for a moment about how you feel—let yourself gradually radiate more self-assurance with each new recitation and word.

Ideally you should do this in a private space so you can be alone with your voice. If you are in a noisy room, head to the bathroom or take a breather outside. If you cannot leave, whisper these words or recite them silently in your head, but make sure your recitation still holds a commanding presence.

PRACTICE POSITIVE AFFIRMATION

Negativity and doubt can strip energy from the mind, but fortunately thinking positively can reverse the damage and shift your mentality.

A great way to encourage optimism is to do a positive affirmation activity. When you do this you're basically using a cheery outlook to promote your self-worth and become more satisfied with your life. This in turn will provide a source of vitality in your life, and your energized brain will start racing about what wondrous things are in store.

How to Practice Positive Affirmation

1. Think of something you love about yourself.
2. Dig deep—is this something unique to you? How does it make you special? Why do you love this attribute in particular?
3. Think of an example of when you expressed this trait. Who did it influence? What was the outcome?
4. Think about how you can use this trait again in the future. Who would it affect?
5. Repeat this activity with a few other traits until your 5 minutes are up. You will feel energized and proud of the type of person you have grown to be.

Give yourself credit for your achievements and positive traits on a regular basis, and you'll noticeably have more energy and liveliness each day.

DO A VISUALIZATION TECHNIQUE

There's something so magical about visualization activities, where you use your imagination to transport yourself to a different place, time, or state of mind to stimulate energy. Using your imagination will increase your creativity and connect you with your feelings and thoughts; it is able to shift your way of thinking and reenergize your mind in just a matter of seconds.

The place you want to visualize is up to you. Pick a moment, an environment, preferred company, an era—*anything*—that will provide positivity, stimulation, and warmth. Close your eyes for the full effect, and let yourself escape momentarily from reality. Here's how to visualize that "happy place":

1. First find a setting that relaxes you. Is it a beach? A vacation home? A park? The mountains? This "happy place" will renew you, hitting all the senses. Let's use the beach as an example.
2. Feel the sand in your toes—the grainy, rough texture that still somehow feels incredibly soft to touch.
3. Listen to the waves crashing and the palm trees swaying in the wind. Feel the warm breeze on your face and in your hair.
4. Smell the seawater or maybe a coconut—something tropical that could be in the vicinity.

Once you're in the midst of visualizing your happy place, take a deep breath, open your eyes, and let the happy feelings you're experiencing energize you for the rest of the day.

TRY SELF-HYPNOSIS

You may be surprised to hear that a great way to refocus the mind is to get lost in hypnosis. This magic spell can give you control over your own thoughts and actions so you can energize the mind in whatever way you choose. Here's how to enter hypnosis:

- Sit down comfortably in a chair, with the thermostat set to a cooler temperature and stillness around you.
- Set a timer for 5 minutes so you can be free of distractions.
- Either immediately close your eyes or pick a point on the wall on which to center your attention.
- Repeat to yourself that your eyelids are getting progressively heavy, to the point where you can't keep them open anymore.
- Take slow, deep breaths.
- Recite a positive mantra that resonates with you, letting it center your mind and speak to your soul. Keep the word or phrase short.
- Repeat this one word or phrase, or choose a few different ones that all hold meaning.
- Keep reciting these affirmations to fill the 5 minutes.
- To come out of hypnosis, slowly count down from ten, telling yourself that once you hit zero, you will open your eyes and be awake.
- Upon reaching zero, say, "Wide awake," or something that orders you to come back to reality.

To make the most of this hypnosis exercise when it comes to building energy, channel it into something positive and spiritual, and have a prepared list of affirmations ready to recite during your hypnosis session. Is there a goal you want to accomplish at work, but you're struggling to stay proactive? Command yourself to work until a certain hour of the day or to hit a particular milestone. Hypnosis will guide you toward achieving your goals and changing your way of thought.

Is there a positive mantra—a word you feel passionate about that can be used in repetition to reinforce positive thought—that you value and need to connect with on a deeper level? Tell yourself to believe in this mantra and to live it to the fullest. Give examples of how you will abide by this mantra and harness its powers. Self-hypnosis is difficult, but with some practice or help from a professional hypnotist, you might be able to accomplish it.

SHARE WHAT YOU LOVE ABOUT SOMEONE

Gratitude and love bring vivacity and energy to your life. They likely remind you of human connection and how meaningful this connection is to your health and happiness. On the opposite side, isolation and loneliness can lead to depression, which will zap the mind of motivation and strength.

Take 5 minutes and single out one person who holds great value in your heart. Write an email, send a letter, send a text message, or actually call your friend or family member to share just how much you care and recognize his or her positive qualities. Touch on a few examples. Is this person reliable? Trustworthy? Fun to be around? Does he or she have a good sense of humor and can make you laugh easily? Is he or she selfless, always looking out for your well-being? Share your appreciation to brighten his or her day as well as yours.

WRITE A PERSONAL LETTER

Jotting down your thoughts and emotions is very therapeutic, and it can re-center and reenergize your mind as you're gathering the right words to express yourself. You can write a personal letter to share with someone else—perhaps your letter involves your relationship or is a letter of gratitude in a friend's honor—or you can write a private letter to yourself. There are a few different ways to go about it:

- Write a letter to your future self. List the things you're looking to accomplish, or give some information on where you envision yourself in a certain number of years. A new job? A raise? A child? In better health? Reconnecting with an old friend? Moving to the city of your dreams? Traveling to another country?
- Write a letter to your present self. Discuss how you're feeling—what's going well in your life and where might you need to improve. Are you happy? What could make you happier right now?
- Write a letter to your past self. Reflect on a behavior from the past. Was it favorable? Unfavorable? How did it affect you? Let it guide you moving forward, learning from example.

The tangible aspect of a letter really validates your feelings and thoughts, so hold the letter in your hand and let its power energize you.

SNAP YOUR FINGERS!

What gets your attention more than a loud snap? Think about it: snapping your fingers in front of your face, directing your eyes to the tips, immediately wakes you up. It's like an alarm has gone off in your head—blink those eyes and look alive! The mere sound of a snap is a jolt, refocusing your attention on the present, and being aware of your surroundings, without distractions, energizes the mind to process, create action, and direct the body accordingly.

The next time you feel yourself drowsing off into la-la land, shock your mind and body with a loud snap of the fingers and see how you feel. You might need to do this a few times in a row if you're extremely weary. After hearing the snap, make a plan. What should you be doing right now? Working? Getting ready to meet friends? Cooking dinner? Putting a child to sleep? Get ready to make some moves.

SCREAM!

Look forward to a fresh beginning and a scream of positive energy! Screaming can be incredibly liberating, and it can help you regain control in your life. First off, screaming is loud—the sheer volume will awaken the mind instantly. Second, when you scream you feel empowered and strong, which can boost your energy levels and motivate you to seize control through the power of your voice. Lift your arms in the air and spread them out to the sides until you resemble a starfish. Throw your head back and look upward. Take a deep breath and let loose! Let the relief overcome your entire body, and feel your mind start to wake up. Repeat until your 5 minutes are up if needed, being sure to take a deep breath in between each scream.

Now you may want to check your surroundings before you begin— clearly screaming at the top of your lungs in your office cubicle or on a busy street might alarm people. If you're in a place where you can't let it all go, you can still scream lightly with your teeth clenched, so it still feels powerful but much more quiet. However, if you are in private and have some space to give the shout your all, go for it! Let out that pent-up tension to let go of worry and fatigue.

PULL YOUR HAIR

We have tons of nerve sensations on our heads. During a massage, the head is a prime area for touch because there's so much stress stored in the mind from anxiety triggers and even just normal thought processes. However, gently pulling the strands of your hair—and feeling that strain come up from the roots—can relieve some of that tension. That pressure on your head will clear your mind and provide focus and stimulation. Here's the best way to perform the activity:

1. Grab a bunch of hair strands, down deep near the scalp, in each hand.
2. Slowly extend the strands outward, in any direction you prefer.
3. Be gentle, and stop pulling once you start to feel that your hair can't extend any farther. Hold here for a few counts, breathing slowly.
4. Repeat this activity for a few minutes, taking a few different strands in your hands each time. Make your way around your head, pulling in various directions. When you're finished with your 5 minutes, gently release your hair strands slowly from your hands. The strands of your hair should feel nice and light.

As the head holds so much strain, playing with your hair and the nerves in your scalp will remove tension and create an energized state of mind.

GET EXCITED!

Excitement, as an emotion, creates momentum, stimulating both the mind and body at the same time. So if you're stuck in a low-energy mindset, think of something that you're looking forward to for that instant energy pick-me-up! When you imagine life's greatest adventures and gifts and think about how they can impact your life, it's hard not to get overzealous and impatient for what's in store. For example:

- Do you have a vacation approaching?
- Are you looking forward to a special occasion, such as an anniversary or a child's birthday?
- Are you in the running for a big promotion at work and can already taste the flavors of that congratulatory cake?
- Do you have plans to catch up with a friend you haven't seen in a while?
- Are you planning to sign up for a new workout class you've wanted to challenge yourself with?
- Is your child in an upcoming school play or recital that you're looking forward to?
- Are you meeting someone for a date who has been fun to chat with over the phone?

Just 5 minutes of this work will provide long-lasting benefits, and you'll have an excited smile on your face for hours after.

LIST FIVE THINGS YOU LOVE ABOUT YOURSELF

There's no better energizer than an ego boost. So give yourself a well-deserved one! Take 5 minutes to list five things that tell yourself just how special you truly are. Even if these qualities aren't what you imagine others would list for you, focus on how you envision your most valuable qualities in your eyes. You can do this in front of a mirror if you prefer, or you can just speak, either silently or out loud, to yourself. These words can be whatever you choose, but make sure they are meaningful to you. This will elicit more energy and feelings of self-worth. Here are a few things to consider as items to note:

1. Think about yourself as a worker. Are you determined? Have you found success on a recent project? Give yourself praise regarding how you handle yourself in your career and what accomplishments you've achieved.
2. Are you a good parent? A caring sibling? Think about your positive qualities in a relationship, and reflect on a way that you've been there for others or have proven valuable in some aspect. Take a deeper look into your character and how it influences others.
3. Consider a quality that makes you who you are. Being authentic and true to yourself can improve vitality for life and energize the mind. This can be related to anything that makes you feel special, unique, and of course, proud of your worth.

You can keep these things that you love to yourself, as something only you recognize and cherish, or you can share them with others, allowing them to experience these positive traits as well.

To go a step further, you can also write down the five attributes you love to always remember them. You can keep these words in a journal and add new entries each day as an energizing activity.

PULL UP A FAVORITE SOCIAL MEDIA ACCOUNT

You don't need to glue your eyes to your social media accounts, and if you feel envious or upset in any way upon looking at others' lives, it's best to avoid it. However, if you have a healthy relationship with your accounts—or those of your friends, spouse, or children—social media can be very energizing and help you take a break from the real world.

Just find a few pages and profiles to follow on sites like *Instagram*, *Snapchat*, *Facebook*, or *Twitter*. There's so much to explore—travel, food, others' happiness, artwork, fashion, and more—so take just 5 minutes to scroll through a popular feed. Maybe look for one that offers entertainment, beauty, knowledge—anything that piques your interest and stimulates your mind. Feel your energy levels soar!

GET ENGAGED IN SOCIAL MEDIA!

While it's fun to look at what other people are doing on social media sites, you can also boost your energy levels by becoming more active on your own social media pages. This lets you use your creativity and mind to think outside the box and design, innovate, and feel connected to others in a vibrant, energetic way.

So head online and post stories, videos, photos, and text about your life that you can share with the world—both your inner world, a network of friends and family who might follow you, and the larger world. (FYI, as your social media pages are public, make sure you're publishing only content you're fine with other people having access to.) Then, an hour or so later in the day when energy is lagging, take 5 minutes to log on and check who's seen your post—look at the likes, views, and comments. Whatever interaction that's present will lift your spirits and energize your mind!

WET YOUR EYES

The eyes need moisture and lubrication to feel awake. If they start to get dry, especially if you have contact lenses, you can feel sleepy. They might even burn and feel uncomfortable and look red and puffy. So if you notice your eyes are tiring, don't let it put your mind to sleep too. Instead, take 5 minutes to dampen your eyes, wipe away excess drops with a tissue, fix your makeup (if needed), and get any dust or dry particles out of there. Blink a few times to make sure your eyes are well lubricated, and move on with your day.

Make sure you're prepared by carrying eye drops in your bag, stashing them in the bathroom cabinet at home, and keeping them in a drawer at your office. You can buy eye drops at any local drugstore, although if you have contact lenses, your doctor might prescribe a brand in particular. Apply every few hours to avoid irritation and to keep your mind awake and alert.

COLOR!

There has been plenty of research on the benefits of coloring for improving cognitive function and decreasing stress and depression. In fact, coloring can reduce symptoms in those with dementia and Alzheimer's disease, as well as those suffering from depression.

Using artistic expression and creativity, along with the imagination, lets the mind act on its curiosity and discover something new. Channeling this fresh stream of energy into productivity can carry over into other areas of life—it will affect work performance, a positive outlook in general, and the ability to think in innovative and out-of-the box ways when it comes to solving problems or juggling multiple tasks. Coloring is also a fun activity that will offer the brain a break when energy levels are getting low.

So take a few minutes to color. It will not only boost your energy levels—and your mood!—in the short term, but it will also enhance your quality of life and mental focus in the long run.

KNIT!

Knitting, which requires great attention to detail, is a fantastic way to get your creative juices flowing, and it focuses your energy on producing something beautiful and intricate. By being more creative, you quickly awaken the mind and boost your energy levels. Since you're using your hands to create knit masterpieces and energize the mind, you will also feel happier, thinking of your inner circle of friends and family for whom you're creating these items. Just imagine those smiling faces when you hand them a winter hat or a pair of socks!

All you need is 5 minutes of knitting time to get the benefits! And don't worry about finishing that blanket for your friend that very day. Knitting can take as much time as you need, because you're able to space it out and fit it into a schedule that's convenient for you. Plus, knitting is accessible—you can carry your tools with you in a bag or stash them at home or at the office.

So get knitting! And start enjoying that energy boost as well!

PLAY AN INSTRUMENT

No matter your natural talents, research has shown that playing an instrument can give an energy boost to both the brain and body, thus promoting happiness, creativity, and productivity. And if you take a few minutes to test your skills, for an audience or just for yourself, you'll get an immediate lift in mood and focus. Plus, if you decide to consistently practice each day, you'll likely improve with time—to the point where maybe you'll want to show off those newfound talents in a public space!

So pick up a guitar, a saxophone, or a set of drumsticks. Play a few chords on the piano. Even carry around a harmonica. Find an instrument that can bring you joy and give you a purpose to learn a new skill set—and enjoy the energy boost that comes along with your newfound talent!

EAT SOMETHING FISHY

Research has long touted the benefits of fish oil and healthy omega-3 fatty acids, found in DHA and EPA, in relation to cognitive function and memory retention. And because these good fats decrease inflammation and power brain function, they can help you stay awake, energized, and focused throughout the day. Omega-3 fatty acids will also improve mood, making you feel happier and more invigorated about life overall.

So how can you get a quick dose of these fatty acids? Take a fish oil supplement that contains a good dose of EPA and DHA in each daily serving! For instance, a requirement of four pills or capsules per serving could indicate it's not worth the same as a supplement with an identical nutritional level in one capsule. Also, read the labels for other ingredients. You want a fish oil supplement that is pure and low in additional fish fat, beyond fat from DHA and EPA.

In addition to this 5-minute fix, try to eat at least three servings of fish a week! All you need to do is one of the following:

- Cook a fish filet for dinner.
- Open a can of salmon or sardines for a quick lunch or salad topper.
- Add smoked salmon to a breakfast bagel or scramble.

Be sure to check for sustainable fish and mercury levels in order to protect yourself from harm. You'll want to keep high-mercury fish, such as yellowfin tuna, to a minimum and opt for low-mercury fish, like salmon, when possible. What's more, eating wild salmon over farmed salmon could be even better, as there's more of these energy-boosting fats and nutrients within.

SNIFF GINGER

Studies have proven ginger's ability to ease cognitive stress, which can then free the mind and create more energy and focus. When there's less tension in the head, it's easier to fight fatigue and feel more awake during the day. Ginger also has anti-inflammatory powers, which fight disease and keep the heart healthy. In addition, it both boosts and maintains the immune system to prevent you from coming down with a case of the sniffles, and it can help mitigate symptoms of nausea and digestive discomfort. Basically, ginger is pretty darn handy to have on hand, especially after eating a big meal where you might feel exceptionally bloated or gassy, because it'll ease the tummy troubles.

How can you get your ginger-fueled energy boost?

- Take a ginger supplement with a big glass of water.
- Rub an essential oil on your pulse points, such as the wrists, temples, neck, behind the knees, and ankles.
- Incorporate fresh ginger into your cooking (think stir-fry vegetables, ginger-glazed salmon, or a refreshing juice or smoothie).

No matter your method, take a few minutes to inhale the smell—it's very strong, so you're going to feel that jolt of energy instantly. You will also smell the ginger in a ginger supplement, just upon opening the container and taking a whiff. Try a few meditative breaths, really savoring the aromas. You'll get an instant kick that will reawaken the mind. For more information on deep breathing techniques, please see "Take a Deep Breath" in Part 1.

Once your 5 minutes are up, close the lid of the supplement or wrap the fresh ginger in plastic wrap and place it in the fridge for later use. This will help the ginger stay fresh so you can get the same full effect in the future. You can also take some ginger scraps to throw into the blender for a juice to take on the go. That way you can have another energy boost later in the day as well as something refreshing to quench your thirst and add a fiery kick to those taste buds. Once you've finished the drink, keep the container with you, as you may be able to still smell the scent of ginger, depending on how much you used in the beverage. Then sniff it throughout the day to stay alert.

SIT IN CHILD'S POSE

Balasana, also known as Child's Pose, is a yoga pose that can energize the mind and body, release tension, and provide greater balance. It's usually a restorative pose that's used in between more challenging poses during a yoga class or session at home, but since it is a great stabilizer exercise, it also maintains that energy flow. It's easy to do and has tremendous benefits on creating vitality throughout the body and boosting circulation. Better blood flow improves energy levels. Here's how to do it:

1. Kneel on the floor, touching your big toes together. Then sit on your heels and expand your knees to about the width of your hips.
2. Breathe and lean forward, laying your body down between your thighs. Lengthen your tailbone by lifting your spine upward and shift the base of your skull away from the neck. You should have full upper body expansion.
3. Extend your arms out in front of you, flat on the ground, and let your shoulders pull your shoulder blades across the width of your back. Breathe deeply in this pose.
4. Once finished, get out of Child's Pose by gently using your hands and walking your torso back to an upright position. Sit back on your heels.

You'll feel refreshed and centered, with more energy to tackle whatever's next on your plate!

DO A PLANK

Planks are often used in exercise classes such as yoga, barre, or HIIT, as they are perfect for strengthening the core and balance. They really work your whole body and especially your mind, since you need to really concentrate to stay in the pose for a minute or so at a time. Plus, you'll get your heart rate up for a moment, but you're not going to start sweating profusely—so you can easily pull out a quick plank midday at work too. What's more, planks teach you how to gain and manage control, which you can use in several areas of your life.

How to Do a Plank

1. Go into a "push-up" position on the ground and bend your elbows 90 degrees, shifting your weight to your forearms.
2. Keep your elbows right underneath your shoulders so your body forms a straight line from head to toes. Don't sink your body inward, but keep it in a straight line, with your hips and stomach flat and stable.
3. Hold for a minute or two.
4. Take a break and stand. Feel the blood flow to your muscles and your brain, increasing your energy levels and keeping you present in the moment. For a greater energy boost, you can do a

few jumping jacks to get that circulation and heart rate up even further.

5. Repeat again.

Doing a core exercise like the plank creates steady energy, which can be used for hours, and it completely resets the body in proper balance.

GO INTO DOWNWARD FACING DOG

Adho Mukha Svanasana, also known as Downward Facing Dog, is great for creating space in the body and stimulating blood flow and circulation, reaching each limb and energizing the mind. This yoga pose requires concentration, but it's very easy to do. You can go into a Downward Facing Dog almost anytime and anywhere.

How to Do Downward Facing Dog

1. Get down on your hands and knees, placing your wrists under your shoulders and your knees under your hips.
2. Inhale deeply and extend your arms until you feel a nice stretch in your elbows, spreading your fingers wide open.
3. Exhale and gently turn your toes inward, underneath your feet, with your heels lifted off the ground. Then lift your knees off the floor and shoot your pelvis up toward the ceiling. Straighten your knees (but be sure not to lock them), and draw your chest toward your thighs, aligning your ears with your arms.
4. Relax your head and neck. Take a few deep breaths in this pose, release, come back up to standing, and exhale. Repeat this exercise for a total of 5 minutes.

Downward Facing Dog is a great position for improving blood flow and energizing the limbs—you'll walk away recharged and awake!

TOUCH YOUR TOES!

Touching your toes not only helps with building flexibility and range of motion, but it also can boost blood flow and get your limbs—and mind!—energized and moving again.

Of course, don't stay too long looking downward at the floor and grabbing those toes, as doing so can make you feel a bit dizzy. Keep this stretch to a few seconds or a minute at a time, and breathe. Let your head hang and feel loose, getting rid of any strain that's in your neck or scalp. Once you come back up to straighten yourself, direct your eyes to a point in front of you and breathe, inhaling and exhaling slowly.

Then repeat! Do this for about 5 minutes for the full effect. If you make a plan to incorporate this exercise each day, your litheness will also improve, which will better your performance during workouts as well.

PLAY A HOME MOVIE

Do you have a favorite family home video that reminds you of happy memories with the ones you love? Take a few minutes and turn it on! These types of visual stimulants will energize your mind and create a positive state of being. Most clips or videos are also very short, and as long as they are stored somewhere safe, like on a computer or phone, you can access them whether you're at home or on the go.

Pick a few videos that help you think positively about life and the wonderful things in it—this could be a family vacation to Greece, a dance recital or soccer game from your youth, or a celebration such as a wedding or an anniversary. You can even store these video recordings in an album or folder, so you can pick whichever type of video you're in the mood to watch without too much thought.

GO INTO CAMEL POSE

Ustrasana, or Camel Pose, is a yoga move that can promote blood flow to your brain and limbs to give both your body and mind an energy boost! This pose works well for easing digestion too, so a great time to do Camel Pose might be after a big meal. You'll also increase your flexibility, get a nice stretch in the front of the body, and release any stress that's in your lower back area.

How to Do Camel Pose

1. Kneel and place your hands on your hips.
2. Keep your heels in line with your shoulders, and let the soles of your feet face upward toward the ceiling.
3. Inhale, and draw your tailbone away from your navel while arching your back and sliding your palms over your feet until your arms are straight.
4. Keep pressure off the neck by keeping it loose and light, maintaining a neutral position—neither flexed nor extended.
5. Take a few deep breaths. While you're coming back up, bring your hands back to your hips and straighten your spine.

Repeat this exercise to fill the 5-minute time frame, and enjoy the energy boost.

SHARE AN ACCOMPLISHMENT WITH SOMEONE

You've done something great? Share it! You don't exactly need to *brag* about yourself, as nobody likes a show-off, but sharing an accomplishment or something you're proud of with someone close to you, like a friend or family member, can energize your mind and provide a lift in happiness. So send a text or call someone to share good news. Since this person cares for you, he or she will probably just be thrilled for you and your success!

Think about a few different areas where you excel—they can be big or small. In fact, if you're doing this each day (hopefully with different people throughout the week!), many accomplishments will be trivial but still hold enough importance to brighten your day. For example:

- Your accomplishment could be related to work—perhaps you finished a grueling assignment or impressed your boss at a meeting.
- Your accomplishment could be something silly and fun—maybe you reached your highest score in a word game or finally learned how to cook pasta the way you like.
- Your accomplishment could be related to your personal relationships—maybe you successfully matched two single friends who really hit it off over dinner.

Use your imagination, and don't be afraid to share your good news! Your mind will thank you!

SHARE AN ADVENTURE!

Take 5 minutes to call or text someone you can count on for a little experimental fun! Taking adventures keeps life interesting, and the novelty of trying something new will provide greater stimulation and a greater energy boost than if you were doing a mundane activity that you're used to.

Our minds are curious and seek thrilling experiences, so make a date to embark on one with someone who will have the right mindset for the adventure. If your buddy has a negative approach, it will hinder the effect. And don't think you need to plan something that's over the top either. Of course, if you want to hike a mountain as an adventure, you sure can, but creating little adventures you can do in the moment will be most helpful in terms of an immediate energy boost. Maybe you can try a new mystery food (what's *jackfruit*, right?) or walk into an old bookstore to see what you can find. Think outside the box!

LOOK IN THE MIRROR!

Staring at your reflection in the mirror is a great way to energize the eyes and focus on something (beautiful) in front of you. When you center your attention on something in front of you, you increase awareness of your surroundings and gain more energy. The fact that you're staring at your own image further motivates you to do *something* productive. It also helps build confidence and creates a connection to your thoughts and feelings, as long as you're thinking positively when glancing at your image.

One way you can help make mirror gazing a positive, energizing experience is to smile while you're looking at yourself. As you learned in the "Smile" entry in Part 1, smiling on its own can boost your energy levels and create feelings of happiness and warmth, thanks to the upturned grin itself, which can instantly wake you up. So be sure to incorporate a smile, along with perhaps a light laugh. Allow yourself to feel liberated and self-assured—let that empowered attitude give you energy to go about your day.

To take your mirror gazing even a step further, practice positive affirmations, which we discussed in the "Practice Positive Affirmation" entry earlier in this part. For example, you might recite a positive mantra, such as "I am strong and bold," while looking yourself in the eye, or you can simply state powerful words, such as "courage," "success," "dominance," or "special." Let these words speak to you and build both your confidence and your energy levels!

CHECK IN WITH AN OLD FRIEND

Take a moment to chat with an old friend who has fallen off your radar. People get so busy—between family life, work stress, and trying to get enough shut-eye—that it's hard to make time for everyone, no matter how much you care for your circle of close ones. Or maybe you and your friend have grown apart in proximity, where perhaps you're living in different cities or time zones, or you just can't see each other as much as you'd like. Just remember it's never too late to rekindle a friendship. And luckily, in today's advanced age of technology, there are many ways to reach people when you can't be together in the same room.

Something as simple as a 5-minute check-in can instantly invigorate you—and your friend—and provide happiness and energy. Plus, these feel-good emotions will last for hours afterward, where your total mental state is reshaped into one that's upbeat and hopeful for the future.

SET A SHORT-TERM GOAL

Something stuck on your to-do list that's stressing you out? Make a plan to get it done in a week's time. This establishment of urgency will motivate you to persevere and finish it. Taking just 5 minutes to strategize will focus your mind and keep it active, set on reaching its target with a method in place.

Create bullet-pointed steps that you'll take on the path to achieving this goal. You can hang your plan on your fridge, keep it on your nightstand so it's the first thing you see come morning, or put it on a sticky note on your desk at work. Keeping this reminder visible throughout the week will increase the likelihood that you'll get it done in the amount of time you've allotted. And if you need more accountability, you can share your goal with someone else who can check in with you regularly throughout the week too.

SET A LONG-TERM GOAL

Think of a goal you have in mind for the future—one you can't achieve right away. Taking just 5 minutes to plan out your goal and come up with a gradual process will give you a big boost of motivating energy and get your mind thinking about the different ways you can achieve your goal. Here are a few suggestions:

1. Do you want to take a vacation somewhere new and exciting? Consider who would join you—friends or family? Or would you go solo? What type of climate do you want? Activities? Duration? What makes this spot so valuable to you, and why might it hold precedence over other places? How will you save money for your trip?
2. Do you want to fall in love? Fall in love again? Find love in other places, beyond a spouse and kids? Think about which relationships you're looking to pursue in order to fill this void and what actions you can take to really put yourself out there and find that love.
3. Do you want to learn a new hobby that requires patience and dedication? Figure out how often you'd need to practice, or by what year you'd like to be able to perform in front of others or show off your talents in some public form.

Let these long-term goals give you the stamina to turn such desires into reality.

WORK ON A BAD HABIT

Nobody is perfect! While you want to energize your mind and fill it with positivity, using constructive criticism to pick out a flaw to work on can actually be a great mental stimulator. And it doesn't have to make you feel bad about yourself! Instead, it will empower you and give you the energy boost you need to be better—to realize you're a great person who is capable of changing flaws because you're courageous, self-aware, and able to achieve whatever you put your mind to.

To start, think of one thing about yourself that you should try to improve. For example:

- Do you have trouble following through on plans?
- Are you too indecisive?
- Do you interrupt people often?
- Are you chronically a tad late?

Then jot down a few points on how to go about making this change in a productive, positive manner. For example, if you struggle to keep plans, make sure to write them down in your calendar, as you would a work event or doctor's appointment. If you think you're indecisive, set a deadline for yourself in making a decision and share that decision with a friend for accountability. Once you've taken just 5 minutes to identify an issue and think of solutions, you'll be motivated to get going! And once you've found success and noticed changes in yourself, you'll feel proud of what you've been able to accomplish.

INDULGE IN A TALENT

Everyone has secret talents they rarely show off. The next time your energy levels have tanked, spend a few minutes relishing *your* talents. The resulting feel-good endorphins will boost your energy and your mood—and the act of practicing your talent is a great way to stimulate your mind.

If you happen to have a talent, such as a beautiful singing voice or magic fingers on the piano, let yourself shine, either alone in your home or in a public place, like a karaoke bar or jazz lounge. If musical talents don't apply, don't fret, but use your imagination. Are you great at solving riddles or puzzles? Can you do a handstand perfectly? Are you savvy in the kitchen? Get motivated to figure out ways to bring joy into your life through an activity you're uniquely proficient in.

PICK UP A MAGAZINE YOU'VE NEVER READ BEFORE

Learning, in general, improves cognitive function and activates the mind, so broaden your knowledge and pick up something you've never considered reading before! There's no reason to stop reading your favorite magazines and newspapers, but looking into a field you're less informed about will provide some major mind perks. Who knows—you might actually enjoy the new selection!

You can head to a local bookstore or browse the Internet for interesting sites, online magazines, and blogs that pique your interest. Set aside 5 minutes to read an article or two. If it's boring, flip to another page or opt for another piece of text that might seem more interesting! There are so many different industries to choose from:

- Politics
- Yoga
- Fitness
- Psychology
- Science
- Art
- Nutrition
- Fashion
- Beauty

Switch it up and aim for variety when doing this activity. That's how you'll get the most energy-boosting benefits since the brain craves originality!

ASK SOMEONE TO LIST YOUR GOOD QUALITIES

It's okay to ask for a little praise and reinforcement every now and then—especially when you know that some complimentary words are going to make you feel good about yourself and give you the energy to make some serious impact on your day! As long as you ask the *right* person for praise—maybe a close friend or family member—he or she probably won't have a problem sharing a few kind words about you.

If you feel insecure asking, try saying, "I'm feeling stuck in my head today. Do you mind telling me something you really like about me?" or something along those lines. Here, your request doesn't come from arrogance, but rather vulnerability. If you so choose, you can write down the qualities for safekeeping, or just listen closely and open your heart to love and the warm vibes.

Let these positive feelings enhance your mood and energy to give you the encouragement you need to get going with your day and make some serious moves.

PART 3

ENERGIZE YOUR MORNING

WAKE UP WITH A FEW BREATHS

There's nothing quite as refreshing as waking up centered and fully awake—which can be especially difficult when that alarm rings at 7 a.m. Instead of jumping out of bed, rest your head on the pillow or sit up with your back against the headboard, and just breathe in and out—inhale and exhale. Let the breath work relax you but also stimulate you and get you ready for the day. Be focused and feel rejuvenated from the night's slumber. (A tip: head to bed 5 minutes earlier to give yourself that time in the morning to do this activity without feeling rushed.)

When life feels hectic, you can find your energy stores depleted. But starting the morning on a relaxed note will empower you for the day ahead. If sitting in bed makes you too sleepy, get up and sit on the floor, with your legs crossed, to do this activity. You can even reset an alarm for 5 minutes, so you won't need to worry about running late and feeling pressed for time to get out the door later.

FIX YOUR HAIR

Take some time to apply some gel, spritz some hairspray, or get dolled up with a braid or updo for a lift in energy. The time and effort that goes into styling your hair will wake you up and require focus, and once it's done, you'll likely feel more confident, which in turn provides energy.

You can also hop in the shower and wash, blow-dry, and style your hair too, but this can't be done in 5 minutes for most women! Men, you can definitely go for that full shower and styling gel. For women, have some fun experimenting with different accessories, tools, and products. You can spend 5 minutes trying a new hair extension, a different dry shampoo, or a curling iron. It's a fun, energizing activity, and it'll let you go to bed knowing you'll have beautiful hair after you wake up.

DRINK WARM WATER AND LEMON

Studies have shown that stable energy levels are one of the benefits of keeping the body in an alkaline state—a pH level of 7 or greater. A body that's too acidic can suffer from low energy, fatigue, and digestive problems, so keeping yours in a healthy, balanced state will allow you to thrive and maintain a better mood and more stamina. One way to keep your pH at an optimal level is to drink a mixture of hot water and lemon juice. The combination creates an alkaline environment in the body (as opposed to an acidic environment), in which the body thrives and contains more energy. The water's heat helps your body absorb the lemon juice and warms the body, releasing tension and creating a greater, energizing balance. Think of this beverage as a morning reset, where you're detoxing your body and making sure it's primed for the day ahead.

So after you've brushed your teeth, showered, and gotten dressed, boil some hot water and squeeze fresh lemon juice into it. If you want, you can add honey too, which is a great purifier and rich in antioxidants. Sip this mixture for a few minutes to really savor the taste, aromas (the smell of citrus has been proven to be invigorating), and overall warmth of the cup. It'll flush the body out and provide a lift in mood and positivity.

SET A POSITIVE INTENTION

A positive intention is a goal that will make a noticeable impact on your energy state and well-being, and it can be something small and easy to attain within a short time frame. Starting your day off with a goal in mind can help steer you in the right direction and get you out the door with a sense of motivation and a mission to get that goal accomplished. This positive intention could be related to a work assignment—perhaps you need to crush a deadline that day or make a great impression during a business meeting with potential clients. It can also be personal, where the goal could be to reconnect with someone over a text message or a phone call, or to get to know someone a bit better.

Whatever the intention, keep it in your mind throughout the day and be sure to write it down, as holding the weight of your intention in your hand can give it even more power and emphasize its urgency. This reminder can go in a notepad, or you can write it on a sticky note to keep in your bag. You can also write it in the notes application on your cell phone to keep track of it and maintain the proper path for the rest of the day. You have only so many hours to accomplish this goal, so a tangible reminder can help you stick with it.

STRETCH YOUR NECK

The neck holds much tension, so relieving that stress first thing in the morning can set you up for a more energetic and enjoyable day ahead. It's really easy to give your neck a good stretch, but be careful not to extend or hold positions for too long, since that can cause strain. You need to know your limits and move slowly, checking in to see if there's any pain. If so, *stop*. Here's a great activity to do:

1. Stand with your feet hip width apart and your arms at your sides. Reach both hands behind your back, using your right hand to hold on to your left wrist.
2. Using the pressure from your right hand, gently straighten your left arm behind you, away from your body.
3. At the same time, move your right ear toward your right shoulder, where you should feel a stretch in your neck.
4. Stay in this pose for 30 seconds. Repeat on the other side, using the left hand to pull the right arm away from your body, moving your left ear toward your left shoulder, and hold for 30 seconds again.

Do this exercise for a total of 5 minutes—you'll leave with a kink-free neck and a little more energy!

POWER UP WITH PROTEIN

Getting some protein into your body first thing in the morning is the best way to wake yourself up and get some staying power! Protein is digested slowly, which gives it the ability to curb your appetite, so while it can provide immediate fuel by boosting your metabolism and getting *something* in your body, it is also long-lasting and will keep you full for hours! When your metabolism is jolted by certain nutrients, such as protein, your body receives newfound energy. There are a few different ways to get a hearty dose of protein in before heading off to work:

1. Whip up some eggs. You can make a scramble, an omelet, a frittata, or even a breakfast burrito. Eggs are rich in protein and choline, which has been proven to improve brain function. You can then add cheese, meats, or veggies to give your breakfast some pizzazz!
2. Have nut butter. Spread some peanut or almond butter on a slice of whole-grain bread. This protein-packed pantry staple is quick and portable too, so you can eat it while heading out the door.
3. Eat lean meat. Breakfast meats that are low in sodium (be sure to check package labels) are high in protein to fill you up, and they can be paired with other protein-dense foods, such as dairy or eggs. Plus, you can prepare a breakfast sandwich the night before so it's ready for a quick zap in the microwave in the morning.

4. Hop on board the avocado craze. There's a reason people are crazy for avocado—whether it's a baked egg avocado recipe or classic avocado toast, you can't go wrong with this creamy, protein-packed breakfast staple. What's more, avocado is high in magnesium, which will brighten your mood and decrease stress levels.

Eating protein every few hours during the day will help you maintain steady energy levels.

SAY "GOOD MORNING" TO SOMEONE

Human contact bright and early in the morning can immediately put you on track for a good day ahead and provide a burst of energy. When you socialize, you release endorphins and relieve stress, which can make you feel invigorated and happier. You can say hello to a partner or child (which is probably easiest, if applicable), or you can text a friend or family member. You can even do this while you're fixing your hair or getting dressed! Studies have shown that human connection can make you feel more alive and excited, and it can also improve health and well-being, thereby resetting the mind and body to create a positive outlook.

Another option is to say hello to someone on the street when you leave your house for the day. It could be on the subway, in a coffee shop, or when you greet a coworker. Then once you settle in for whatever your day has in store, you'll be in a great mood, eager to tackle your first task of the day.

DRINK SOME COFFEE!

If you do wake up a bit groggy—which is pretty normal, so don't be worried—a hit of java could be just what you need. Coffee has caffeine, which speeds the metabolism and provides a jolt of energy to mentally and physically wake you up.

When pouring a cup of coffee, go easy on the milk or cream and the sugar—too much can slow you down and be a major calorie bomb in disguise. To reap the maximum amount of energizing benefits, drink your coffee black or add a dash of milk and natural sweetener, such as stevia or agave. However, trying to wean yourself off the sugary taste entirely can be helpful, since it will change your taste buds and train you to desire less sugar overall. (For more information on the dangers of excess sugar, read "Ditch the Sugar" in Part 1.) Also, be sure to time your cup of coffee right—you don't want that caffeine kick to go to waste or get you too jittery.

To get the maximum perk, avoid peak cortisol hours, which take place between 8 a.m. and 9 a.m. and again from noon to 1 p.m. Cortisol is the stress hormone, which can zap energy levels and weigh you down. Drinking coffee during these time frames will create more anxiety in the mind and body, which can be draining and cause those caffeine benefits to backfire. So grab a cup midmorning instead. And it's worth noting that if you like to have coffee again in the afternoon to avoid that afternoon slump, cut yourself off before 5:30 p.m. and wait until

6:30 p.m. as cortisol spikes again for another hour. That said, drinking caffeine too late in the day can interfere with your circadian rhythm and prevent you from falling asleep, so be mindful of its particular effects on you. Without adequate sleep, you'll wake up fatigued, which will make energizing your morning (even with that cup of coffee) a whole lot harder.

Of course, if you are sensitive to caffeine or don't like the taste of coffee, there are other alternatives. These include lower-caffeine teas, such as green or white tea, or a bite or two of dark chocolate to wake you up. (The darker the concentration of the dark chocolate, the higher the antioxidant count, which will further promote feel-good sensations.) Whichever way you choose to get your caffeine kick, you're sure to feel more energized once you do! Just stick to about 300 milligrams to 400 milligrams of caffeine a day for terrific energy without going overboard.

GET YOUR HEART RATE UP

Getting out from under your covers can be a struggle if you're sluggish and low in stamina, and that fatigue can carry over into your morning hours too. However, if you start your day with a 5-minute workout, you can instantly shock your body—mind, muscles, and heart rate—to not only get that immediate energy boost and wake up *fast* but also burn calories and get fitter with time. To energize yourself to get out from under those covers, set your alarm to a favorite song or a tune that offers motivation to hop right into your day. It'll give you the proper mindset to want to exercise and wake up the rest of your body. Then you can work out within a minute or two of getting out of bed. Throw on your workout clothes, brush your teeth, and begin.

Do whatever appeals to you—it can be higher-intensity work, cycling, the treadmill, or the elliptical (if you have access to a gym), or you can just do some squats to get your body moving and blood flowing. You can even just go for a brisk walk outside or take your pup out for a quick bathroom break. Deciding what type of activity to do is a matter of preference and activity level. Any little bit will help in jolting you out of dreamland!

WINK AT YOURSELF

This activity might sound silly, but it's foolproof! Winking builds confidence, as it's a sensation that can make you feel sexy, in control, and alive—all of which can supply immediate energy and even reshape your whole mental state for a positive day ahead. So look in the mirror and give yourself a good wink. You can even add on to this by saying, "Hey there, good looking" or "You're looking like a star today." It's a great way to feel good about yourself and get yourself eager to get outdoors and let your radiance shine. Plus, it's quick and easy to do—you don't need to stare at yourself winking for hours in order to get the benefits.

If you feel embarrassed, do this in private. That means if your spouse, child, or coworker is sharing a bathroom with you, hold off. Wait for that person to exit and then compliment yourself, however you may choose. Just remember, though, that there's nothing to be embarrassed about here—you deserve to acknowledge how awesome you are!

HOP IN THE SHOWER

Did you know that a morning shower can wake you up? It literally wipes out the sleep from your eyes! For the majority of the shower, make sure that the water isn't superhot, but rather right in the middle or even on the cooler end, which is ideal. (For your skin too—hot water can dry it out.) Then at the end, finish off with a blast of cold water for a few seconds before stepping out. Studies have shown that manipulating temperatures, such as going from warm to cold, may raise energy levels by shocking the body's system and shifting between two extremes. Taking 5 minutes for a quick shower will instantly shock the body and energize the mind.

To take it further, when you're in the shower, make it enjoyable and worthwhile. Sing your favorite song, lather up with an invigorating scented bodywash, or think about how great the day will be once you hop out and towel off.

MAKE A TO-DO LIST

If you're anxious about which tasks to prioritize for the day or you're worried that you won't get to everything in time, take a few minutes first thing in the morning to make a to-do list of the tasks you need to complete during the day—and stop driving yourself crazy! Once your to-dos are written down, you'll have a clear idea of which direction you need to go in order to achieve your most immediate goals, and the reassurance that you're one step closer to finding success will energize you to try to achieve those goals with greater urgency. Simply create a bullet-pointed list of the items that you need to tackle, and list a deadline for each. The need to finish in a given period of time prevents procrastination and provides the energy needed to take action fast. Does a report need to be finished by 3 p.m.? Write that down, and list it above "make dinner for the family," which could have a later extension of 6 p.m. or 7 p.m. instead.

Keep this checklist on hand during the day so you can monitor your progress. Once you've completed something, check it off and move on to the next item. It'll feel great to see the items vanish, and you'll start off the morning feeling prepared—with a focused, determined, energized attitude that will lead you to success!

THINK OF SOMETHING THAT SCARES YOU

Studies have shown that fear and urgency can be a powerful motivator and energizer, so think of something that scares you to get yourself in gear for the day ahead. How does it work? Well, fear adds a time line or obstacle into the equation that can force you to problem-solve and make moves fast.

Are you scared of losing a client? Use this fear as motivation to finish an assignment for the client today or to schedule a coffee date or check-in. Are you worried about botching your best man's speech at your brother's wedding? Come up with a few jokes that are sure to be crowd-pleasers, and write them down so you don't forget them. Or is it a long-term fear, such as not getting a promotion you've been working for? Use this worry to motivate yourself to really impress your boss that day—come up with a game plan upon entering the office that morning.

Don't get too carried away here, though—you don't want to be frightened to the point where you have a defeatist attitude or fall apart. To prevent this, remind yourself that your thoughts and actions will lead you to a positive outcome, and stay levelheaded with stable energy and focus during this exercise.

SET YOUR ALARM TO A SONG

Instead of waking up to the loud, aggressive sound of the alarm, wake up to an upbeat song instead! You can pick a song that's a top hit or on a feel-good playlist, or you can choose an upbeat alarm option that can still empower you to throw off those sheets and get out the door wide awake and ready to start the day.

Take a few minutes to browse through a collection and find an alarm setting that works for you. Then, each morning when you hear it, you'll immediately have a better state of mind and be in a more positive mood. Plus, you can change up the setting throughout the week if you want. Sometimes routine can get boring, and that variety can add extra stimulation. To find a song, ask for recommendations from friends or browse online. Experiment with a few songs and see what brings about positive energy. You can then set this song as the alarm on your phone or use a radio alarm, depending on your preference.

HAVE A GREEN JUICE!

Green juices (juices that contain several leafy greens, such as spinach or kale, and are lower in fruit and sugary items) are great for detoxing the body and clearing toxins, and they are really refreshing and energizing first thing in the morning. Because of the fast-acting carbs from the vegetables and nutrients such as calcium and iron, your mind and body get an instant jolt of energy, and if there's any fiber in the juice, you'll also stay fuller longer. Keep in mind, though, that when it comes to the benefits of drinking juice, it's all about the ingredients. If your juice is high in sugar and doesn't contain enough green vegetables, it could lead to a crash later in the day. If you're making your own, throw in a few green or nonstarchy vegetables and then pick a fruit or two, or a fruit and a starchy vegetable if you like. It's all about proportions. If you're looking for an energy-boosting combo, try one of the following:

- Spinach, lemon, kale, and kiwi
- Carrots, turmeric, spinach, Swiss chard, and ginger
- Blueberries, kale, spinach, Swiss chard, and banana
- Watermelon, kale, Swiss chard, mint, and blackberries
- Apple, spinach, kale, mint, lemon, and cucumber
- Beets, Swiss chard, celery, cucumber, apple, and ginger

If you're buying a packaged juice from a store, check the label and serving size—most have a serving size of two, so double that sugar count before thinking it's okay. As long as your juice is healthy, it can boost your mood and provide the right set of nutrients to energize your mind and fuel your brain, helping you feel more alert. Plus, they taste pretty good, which is always an added perk!

HAVE A SHOT OF APPLE CIDER VINEGAR

Apple cider vinegar might taste bitter, but the benefits are real! Studies have shown that waking up to a shot of apple cider vinegar can reset the body and mind into an alkaline, or less acidic, state and get rid of toxins, providing energy. It can also cleanse the system, which can help prevent damage from toxic elements over time. Plus, it's said to stabilize blood sugar, so it'll prevent any swings that could drain energy, and it'll keep your body in a balanced, high-functioning state.

If you don't like the taste, you don't need to drink apple cider vinegar straight to get the benefits! You can easily dilute it with water to make it taste better going down. Add 1 to 2 teaspoons of apple cider vinegar to 8 ounces of water (a glass of water), and take it before eating your breakfast. Or if you're new to apple cider vinegar, try 2 teaspoons of apple cider vinegar with one teaspoon of honey swirled in water, and see how you feel.

EAT GREEK YOGURT

Greek yogurt is rich in protein to give you an energy boost and encourage satiety, so you'll stay full for the next couple of hours. However, that's not the only benefit—it's also a great source of probiotics, which can improve gut health and smooth digestion. By eating Greek yogurt early in the day, you're immediately setting yourself up for greater energy and digestive comfort. And the way you begin your day can really influence how the rest of it goes.

What's more, probiotics keep you regular—meaning you'll go number two as often as you should—and they balance out the body, so mood and energy levels are stable and good bacteria can thrive in the gut. How amazing is it that Greek yogurt has *both* protein and probiotics for double the energy boost?

You can eat Greek yogurt with any of the following ingredients:

- Fruit
- Nuts
- Seeds
- Berries
- Dark chocolate
- Granola
- Olive oil

These add-ins can give your plain yogurt a bit of sugar and flavor without overdoing it!

GIVE LOX SOME LOVE

Lox is smoked salmon—it's absolutely delicious and gives you a great morning energy boost! Smoked salmon is high in omega-3 fatty acids, which can improve heart health and cognitive function while reducing inflammation in the body. These fats, made up of DHA and EPA, energize the mind and body to help you be more productive and alert.

Beyond the concentration of fats, smoked salmon also has a lot of protein, which provides energy and creates fullness in the body. However, be mindful of portion size, as smoked salmon is pretty high in sodium.

How can you add lox to your diet? Try the following!

- Spread on toast or a bagel
- Mixed with eggs for a light and fluffy omelet or scramble
- In a salad with burrata cheese and spinach
- Inside an avocado along with cheese or other vegetables, such as radishes and asparagus
- As a source of good fats and protein to go with a bed of lentils and arugula

If you are opting for the bagel or toast, make sure you're using whole-grain or whole-wheat varieties, as these have fiber to fill you up and not spike blood glucose levels, which can lead to fatigue later.

MAKE PLANS!

Start your morning off with some excitement for what's to come later that evening. If you have fun plans, such as a dinner with friends, a happy hour, or a movie night with the family, you're going to have something to look forward to. When you're eager for the day's agenda, you'll feel energized to get moving out the door!

Here's what to do. Call or text a friend, or chat with your family, about meeting up later. Make a plan. If one person is busy, try another. Spend a few minutes connecting with someone who is available and setting something up.

Even if you don't have a specific activity in mind, just get something on the docket. There's plenty of time to figure out the logistics later.

BOOK AN EXERCISE CLASS

Exercising is a great way to boost your energy, mood, and mind, and it's a chance to free yourself from any built-up tension or stress that's weighing heavily on your mind. This is a time to sweat, feel strong, and focus on *you*. You can work out alone or invite a buddy—it's up to you. Some people feel as though having others there for support holds them accountable, so if you find it hard to motivate yourself to get to the gym, this could be a great solution.

If you book a class right in the a.m., you'll know you're going to have a major calorie burn later, which will motivate you to avoid a lazy mentality during the daytime. Knowing you're going to be a warrior helps you become one—so there's no reason not to start early in shaping that mindset.

DO JUMPING JACKS

Earlier in this part we already discussed how getting your heart rate up can energize your morning, and jumping jacks let you do that while having a little fun! Jumping jacks are good for any fitness level, and you can always go at your own pace and intensity too. They're so easy to do anywhere; you can do them at home right upon getting out of bed, in the kitchen when preparing breakfast for yourself or your family, or even upon reaching the office (you can do them in your cubicle, your private office, the bathroom, or the stairwell).

Give yourself 5 minutes to do jumping jacks—but feel free to take breaks. You can try an EMOM workout, which stands for "Every Minute on the Minute," meaning you'll do jumping jacks for 1 minute, then rest for 1 minute, and repeat until you've covered the whole 5 minutes. The great thing about this setup is you can give yourself enough time to work hard and recover, and it'll train you to need less and less recovery time the more you practice.

CHECK YOUR MAILBOX!

Before heading off to work, check your mailbox to see if you received anything important. First off, it gets your feet moving, as you physically need to go outside to the mailbox or mailroom downstairs. Second, it's something to look forward to or check off your list.

- Let's say you have an unexpected invitation to an event, such as a wedding. This can instantly bring positivity to your day.
- Have bills to pay? Take a minute to write a check or pay online. Then you can breathe a sigh of relief and know that you don't need to worry about that in the future. Knowing there's one less issue to deal with will surely energize you!
- See if you got any mail that's just for you! Everyone loves to receive a personalized note in the mail or a surprise package—this can be a huge mood booster. Next step? Rip open the package or letter and see who it's from! Send a thank-you note or email, if necessary.

Just because a lot of correspondence is online doesn't mean some good, old-fashioned snail-mail can't bring about a different form of energy to uplift your spirits.

BRUSH YOUR TEETH

Wake up by energizing your mouth! Brushing stimulates saliva production, which can boost alertness, and if you're choosing a peppermint toothpaste, you'll get double points, since peppermint has been shown to improve mental function and focus. The act of refreshing your mouth will in turn refresh your mind and body, and you'll feel ready for the day ahead.

Don't brush too hard, but brush enough so you're adding the right amount of pressure and covering all your teeth. You should be cleaning your tongue, gums, and teeth for about 2 minutes total to keep your mouth healthy and promote better hygiene.

You can make brushing your teeth more fun by putting on music. Playing a few tunes in the bathroom as you get ready can make the morning more enjoyable, and it'll make something as mundane as brushing your teeth feel more lively and upbeat. Pick a song that lasts about 2 minutes (the amount of time needed to adequately brush your full set of teeth). It shouldn't be hard—most songs last for longer! To tack on a few minutes, you can then floss or use mouthwash. In this case, have another song ready—perhaps on a "brushing teeth" playlist!

GARGLE WITH WATER

Start your morning off right by gargling with either plain water or salt water. Either one will work—it just depends on your preference! Gargling can give you a lift in your energy level since it's increasing saliva in your mouth, which can stimulate the mind and prevent dehydration. (Dehydration, in turn, has been shown to cause fatigue.) What's more, the auditory aspect of gargling can further alert the mind and body since it's pretty loud and can help you stay alert and present. Plus, if you do choose to gargle with salt water, the salt can purify and detoxify your mouth, tongue, and gums, and the salty, pungent taste will help perk you up!

You can also gargle with mouthwash in a peppermint or cinnamon flavor. Research has shown that peppermint and cinnamon can improve mental focus and blood circulation, both of which can lead to steady energy levels. (Learn more about the benefits of peppermint in the "Chew Peppermint Gum" entry in Part 2.) Take about 2 minutes to gargle and spit. Then smile in the mirror and admire your fresh, clean pearly whites!

EAT A BANANA

When you sleep, you're more prone to sweating, even if you keep your thermostat at a low, comfortable temperature. And when you sweat, you lose electrolytes, which your body needs to stay balanced and keep fatigue at bay. So when you wake up and have depleted these mineral stores, your body desperately needs hydration and potassium to rebuild the deficit and regain energy. A banana is the perfect breakfast food. It is high in potassium, which works to rebalance the electrolytes in your body and provide steady energy, and it has a good amount of fast-acting carbohydrates, which can give you an immediate perk.

To add more protein and satiating fat to your breakfast, try the following!

- Add some banana slices and nuts to Greek yogurt.
- Spread mashed bananas on a slice of whole-grain toast with nut butter.
- Blend a banana in a protein-packed smoothie that you can take on the go. This smoothie should have some fats, protein, and greens to go with the banana. As for liquid, coconut water could be a great choice because it's high in potassium and electrolytes.

This way, you'll get those energizing benefits and a tasty treat all in one.

ENJOY YOUR COMMUTE

While your commute will inevitably take more than 5 minutes to complete—at least in most cases—you can still take a few minutes to come up with a way to make the rest of it feel less like a burden. Maybe you can actually make it fun! Do whatever you need to do to perk up your commute so you can bring your energy levels up, rather than stay stuck in that morning sleepiness. Here are some suggestions for improving your trek to work for an easier and more energized morning:

- If you're biking to work, stop yourself every few blocks to do an additional quick, more focused exercise. For example, you can do a few push-ups on the handlebars. This will create more energy and blood flow in your arms and shoulders specifically.
- If you're on the train, bring your headphones and listen to music! This will make your morning happier and more invigorated. Find a playlist that gets your day going and brings positivity. You can also choose to strike up a conversation with a stranger sitting near you—however, be sure to gauge the person's attitude first. If the stranger is working or listening to music, he may not want to talk to you. Just don't take it personally!
- If you're in the car, you can always listen to music, but take it a step further and listen to a great speech, one that's empowering and can motivate you for the day ahead! You can also turn on a

podcast that you find interesting. You can even listen to an educational program to learn a new skill such as a foreign language, which will stimulate your mind and provide a burst of energy.

- If you're walking to work, take a 5-minute detour and discover a new area. Walk into a store and peek around, or just keep walking with your eyes and ears open, taking in all the new experiences. Find beauty in buildings, see if there's an intriguing shop you'd like to visit in the future, or check out the menu of a restaurant that looks right up your alley. Take this time to explore and indulge your senses, and maybe even jot down a few places or snap a few photos so you'll know where to return.

There's no need to slowly trek to work with a sluggish mindset when it's easy to incorporate energizing activities on your morning commute!

EAT GRAPEFRUIT!

Grapefruit, which is in the citrus family, has been shown to improve energy states for many reasons, and it tastes great too! The scent alone has been proven to improve your mental alertness and enhance your mood. Eating the fruit can also help suppress appetite, so when you eat it for breakfast, you'll feel fuller in the day and be less likely to crave sugary, refined foods that can cause you to lose steam early.

Half of a medium grapefruit, which is a proper serving size, is all you need to get these benefits. You can pair the grapefruit with other foods that will add a dose of protein and good fats as well. For instance, pair grapefruit with a cup of Greek yogurt, ricotta, or cottage cheese for protein and calcium. And throw in some almonds or pistachios for added fats. If you feel that grapefruit is too tart for your tastes, you can make it sweeter or more savory, depending on your preferences. For instance, drizzling honey and pistachios can make it sweeter, while adding basil or cilantro will give it a savory edge.

Beyond eating grapefruit, you can also buy a grapefruit-scented lotion or bodywash to use in the morning. This will invigorate the body and smell nice—which is just an added perk!

TAKE A PHOTO OF THE OUTDOORS

Nature can be stimulating for both the mind and body, and research has found that beauty and natural elements can boost energy levels as well as relieve tension and stress, create a positive outlook and mental state, and enhance overall well-being. And here's even more good news! Nature can be found everywhere, no matter where you live. Even cities have parks and recreational spaces to frequent during the day! Just think of how beautiful the trees and leaves can be throughout the seasons' changes. Plus, there are even gardens and outdoor farmers' markets you can visit.

To start your morning on a high note, either head outside to take a photo in person or snap one from your home window. If you wake up at sunrise, you can get a really unique and beautiful shot of the sky, with different colors and a stillness that's peaceful and rejuvenating! You can keep it for yourself and admire it on your computer or phone, or you can upload it to social media and share it with others. If you choose the latter option, have some fun experimenting with different filters and features to make the photo even more personalized.

WATER THE PLANTS

There's something so wonderful about having fresh plants in the house, especially in the morning when you're looking for a way to connect to the world and its beauty. You can experience an energy boost just by feeding off the energy plants can give. Plants are living creatures that need to be watered and tended. Taking 5 minutes in the morning to water your plants and flowers can be very relaxing and enhance your mood, and it'll keep them alive and well.

Even just having fresh plants in the house can keep you invigorated for life. Staring at something beautiful and appreciating its worth is in our DNA—that's why babies stare at beautiful objects and faces. They are naturally drawn to these things and then, of course, let out a smile and giggle. Much like children, adults like to surround themselves with visual stimulation and splendor, and flowers have all of these qualities while also connecting us to the earth and giving us that much-needed energy boost.

EAT AN APPLE

Apples are full of complex carbohydrates and sugars, which provide immediate, fast-acting energy, but they're also high in fiber, which will help you avoid the dreaded carb crash. Why? The fiber in apples offers slow-digesting advantages, meaning they will keep you full for hours and stabilize your blood sugar levels for greater, more balanced energy. This way you'll avoid an energy crash later and won't have to worry about dealing with sugar cravings.

Plus, apples make a satisfying crunch when eaten, and research has shown that crunchy foods, such as apples, carrots, and celery sticks, can freshen your breath and mouth and clean your teeth! The crunchy sound itself can also make you more alert in the present moment, as a "crunching" sound is jolting by nature. Besides, fresh fruit in the morning can curb any sugar craving you might have upon waking up (think—a doughnut!), so you can eat something that's high in natural sweetness and way healthier instead.

HAVE A SHOT OF MATCHA

Matcha—powdered green tea leaves—contains caffeine and antioxidants that are perfect for giving you that morning energy boost! If you don't like the taste of coffee or if you find the caffeine content to be too strong, matcha is a great alternative. It's a bit lower in caffeine than coffee but still has enough to get those energizing benefits. Plus, those antioxidants have been shown to lower inflammation, which protects your brain and keeps it stimulated.

There are many proven benefits to matcha! The caffeine and antioxidants in each cup improve your cognitive function and focus, and even help increase your productivity by keeping you alert. The powers of antioxidants go beyond energizing the mind and reducing inflammation in the body: they can also prevent disease, such as heart disease, brain disease, and even cancer, and they can directly improve your health and happiness by fighting depressive symptoms and anxiety.

Matcha can also aid in weight loss and maintenance, as well as in maintaining high energy, by speeding the metabolism and keeping it elevated for hours. When the metabolism is revved, there's more available energy. So if you're looking for a metabolic boost in the a.m., that shot of matcha can do the trick.

CLEAN YOUR EARS!

Cleaning your ears with a cotton swab can instantly provide a kick of energy, as the process of cleansing and the pressure on the eardrum will wake you up and make you feel more alert. The auditory sensation of putting pressure on the eardrum stimulates wakefulness, as it makes you aware of what you're doing and your surroundings with a clear focus. What's more, this act of personal hygiene, in itself, provides reassurance that you're eliminating toxins bright and early. That feeling of freshness can symbolically energize you—it's like a new beginning, without debris weighing you down. However, be careful not to go too deep when getting rid of that buildup of wax in there. Pushing too hard can be dangerous to the interior of the ear, causing a rupture or tear. Likewise, having a bit of wax is healthy, since it protects the ear from pathogens and other toxins that can enter the body.

Be sure to clean your ears once a week or every few days. It's not necessary to clean them each day, as there's not going to be enough wax to remove. If there's a lot of dark wax, it might mean you're not cleaning regularly enough, and you could benefit from cleaning your ears more frequently. If you are concerned, you can always speak to a doctor to discuss the best schedule for you.

SPRAY PERFUME OR COLOGNE

Wake up on the bright side with a sniff of your favorite scent, which can energize you inside and out! The power of smell is important in creating a state of mind and bodily sensations, and if you choose a scent that is linked to a pleasant memory or specific positive emotion, it can shape your mood and boost your energy for the day ahead. Besides, when you're looking for a reminder midday, the scent will still be lingering on your wrists, neck, and hair.

You can even choose a perfume or cologne that makes you feel confident and secure. Allow it to empower you to accomplish something on your to-do list or ask someone for a favor you've been dreading to mention. A bold scent is sure to leave a strong impression on your attitude and maybe even on those around you. Think of it as your own personal scent—one that exudes your true, positive qualities.

SNAP A SELFIE

While you don't need to share your selfie on social media or with friends or family, snapping a photo of yourself in the a.m. can make you feel confident and energized for the day ahead. It's a great way to let yourself shine and to acknowledge the fact that you deserve to have your picture taken—a beautiful one, at that.

You can take whatever type of photo you want. It can be an authoritative photo, perhaps where you're upright or posing with a calm, collected, and composed demeanor. Or it can be a silly shot, where you might be sticking your tongue out, laughing, or doing something playful and fun with a huge grin on your face.

You can even take a few different photos, touching on various emotions and themes, for a mini photo shoot to get you pumped for the next few hours.

DRINK A SMOOTHIE

Smoothies are not just a great way to get easy fuel when you're on the go in the morning! They're usually prepared in a blender, and the loud noise of a blender first thing in the morning is bound to jolt your mind into waking up! In addition, they are packed with nutrients and protein—if they consist of the right type of ingredients. Protein creates energy in the body, as it activates the metabolism. And the other nutrients typically found in smoothies, like fiber, antioxidants, and magnesium, also improve energy levels, as the foods containing them provide both fast-acting and slow-acting carbohydrates for instant and stable energy.

When it comes to making a smoothie, you'll want a good balance of healthy fats, vegetables and fruit, protein, and fiber. All of these work together to build satiety and create long-lasting energy. Also, pectin, which is a source of fiber, is found on the skins of fresh produce, like kiwi, apples, and pears. So be sure to keep the skin on! No sure what to drink? Here are a few suggestions.

Energizing Smoothies

- **Berry Antioxidant Smoothie:** Blueberries, blackberries, spinach, hemp seeds, and unsweetened almond milk or Greek yogurt. Berries are high in antioxidants, which can boost brain health and improve memory retention, and yogurt, hemp seeds, and almond milk provide protein to speed the metabolism and give you that energy boost.

- **Peanut Butter Banana Smoothie:** Think of how great peanut butter and a banana taste together, and start your morning with a smoothie featuring this dynamic duo! Add unsweetened almond milk and sneak in some kale or spinach if you can. You can also use a chocolate protein powder for some sweetness and more staying power. Bananas are high in electrolytes and magnesium to prevent dehydration and fatigue, which will help energize you bright and early.
- **Green Smoothie:** Better than green juice, this green smoothie has way more protein and healthy fats to keep you full for longer. Use kiwi (skin included), kale, spinach, vanilla protein powder, unsweetened almond milk, spirulina, chia seeds, and banana. The chia seeds have healthy fats that power your metabolism to improve energy and increase fullness, while kiwi's fiber will provide both immediate and sustained energy for the next few hours.
- **The "Dessert" Smoothie:** There's nothing wrong with some chocolate in the morning! Add dark chocolate or cocoa nibs, nut butter, coconut, unsweetened almond milk, berries, and yes, spinach or kale. The chocolate and nut butter will easily mask the taste of the greens, and you'll still get the benefits, such as iron, calcium, and fiber. Here you'll feel energized from the hit of caffeine and antioxidants from dark chocolate—no coffee needed.

All of these smoothies will taste great and provide wonderful energizing benefits to hold you over until your next meal.

EAT ESPRESSO BEANS

Espresso beans give an instant hit of caffeine-created energy, so pop one or two when you don't have time to make yourself a cup of coffee or when you're looking for something with a stronger flavor! Caffeine has been shown to make you less drowsy, so eating espresso beans could be especially helpful if your morning routine involves a car ride. You don't want to get sleepy at the wheel!

You can buy espresso beans at any grocery store or coffee shop, and you can even find some espresso beans covered in dark chocolate. These will taste even better, and the dark chocolate provides a nice source of caffeine to energize the mind and body.

GIVE SOMEONE A KISS

Whether you live with a partner or a house full of children, find someone to kiss upon waking up and heading out the door. Studies have shown how powerful love and human connection are on energy levels and happiness, so if you're high on these measures, you'll be more invigorated to get out the door and do something productive with your day.

What's more, kissing is a form of intimacy that can elicit feel-good feelings and hormones such as oxytocin, which is released when we engage in human touch and closeness. Oxytocin directly improves mood, which will make the morning feel brighter and more hopeful.

Your kiss doesn't need to be long—just a quick peck on the lips, head, cheek, or hand will do the trick. Plus, if you're kissing a loved one in your home, the level of affection is bound to be reciprocated, which will bring even more positivity, joy, and energy to your life—and theirs too!

INDULGE IN SOME WISHFUL THINKING

Start your day by giving yourself something to look forward to! You can pick one wish or a couple, but be sure to flesh it out and explain why you want it to happen, how it will affect you and your life in the short term or long term, and what you can do to turn it into reality.

Of course, your wish doesn't need to be a realistic goal or something to check off your to-do list. This can actually be totally fictitious or silly—it can be a fantasy of something you hope will happen, unexpectedly, on a given day. This aspect of hope and the possibility of surprise will get you geared up and ready to see what the day has in store for you. However, remember that wishful thinking is just a positive activity to get you energized—so don't be disappointed if your day ends without having accomplished what you wanted to happen.

STRETCH YOUR FEET

After lying in bed for hours, your feet could be sore or stiff. In fact, it could take a few minutes for your feet to adjust once you stand up—especially the heels, which can be a source of pain for many people. If you happen to wear heels or uncomfortable shoes during the day, your feet could be even more sensitive. Similarly, your feet could be extra achy if you have plantar fasciitis, which can cause sharp pain in the heels extending throughout the midpoint of the foot to cover the arch. It is at its worst after long periods of time without movement, such as being in a chair for hours or first thing in the morning.

A solution? Do a few foot exercises to wake your body up, ease any pain, and just get some new blood circulating throughout your limbs to encourage activity and momentum!

Some Foot Exercises to Try

- Do calf stretches. Usually when feet are tired, it's likely that the calves are tight too, which can cause added pressure on the feet. Do some calf stretches by placing your hands against a wall and pressing your body weight into it for 1 minute, with one leg pushed straight back and the other bent, as if you were in a forward lunge. Lean your body weight toward the wall to really feel that stretch in the extended leg and calf. Do this with a 30-second hold, then switch legs. Repeat on the other side.

- Stretch your toes as wide as they can go, letting them separate from one another to widen the whole foot. Feel that stretch, and hold for a few seconds. Bring your toes back to their resting state, and then repeat for a couple of rounds.
- Sit in a chair and lift one leg to rotate your ankle in a circular motion. First, flex your foot and let the arch expand, stretching the toes wide apart. Then rotate your ankle, and crunch your toes into the sole of your foot. This will increase circulation all around and improve flexibility. Circle ten times and then repeat with the other ankle.
- Rub your heels. Dig into those heels with your fingers and break up knots that could be causing pain or tightness from daily use. Your feet do so much—there's bound to be some pent-up tension! Make your way to the arch from the heels, giving yourself a good massage with enough pressure to alleviate any stress that's weighing on your feet. You can also use a golf ball or massage roller designed specifically for the feet.

Do these exercises for a total of 5 minutes, either picking just one or doing a sequence of exercises to target different areas.

SIP KOMBUCHA!

Kombucha—a type of carbonated, fermented tea (often black or green)—is made of probiotic-rich bacteria, which has been shown to improve energy levels and help regulate and balance the gut by producing good bacteria strains and eliminating bad ones that can hinder digestion. Kombucha gives an even more intense energy boost than taking other types of probiotics! Be wary of its consistency—it might take some getting used to. It's flavored and has a strange, bubbly texture that can feel odd on the tongue. However, this atypical sensation will wake you up, as its carbonated, fizzy consistency is stimulating to the mouth.

You can drink kombucha plain—many stores offer packaged kombucha-based beverages that have different flavor profiles, such as berry or a spicy cayenne—or you can even incorporate it into your favorite breakfast dish. Many people use kombucha to create dressings and vinaigrettes, which can be delicious atop morning eggs or greens.

MAKE YOUR BED

Right after jumping (or slowly moving) out of bed, take 5 minutes to make your bed so it'll be neat and tidy when you return to it that night. Not only will the process of straightening up help you get moving and feel more alert to start the day, but it also will make you feel more organized and prepared in general. Studies have shown that your living and organizational habits can shape your productivity and stress levels, so by keeping your space clean and orderly, you'll have a more positive outlook and be able to accomplish much more in the day.

Be sure to fold any covers and comforters, and place all pillows on the bed. You can either keep your pajamas out, folded nicely on the bed or placed under your pillow, or place them in a drawer. And even though this activity will help wake you up in the a.m., it will make your evening a lot easier too! There's nothing better than being able to just hop into bed right when you're dozing off and primed for a good night's sleep.

USE THE RESTROOM

When you sleep at night, your body works hard to digest the food you've eaten during the latter part of the day and the evening. This means that when you wake up in the morning, you may have to use the restroom to excrete any waste that's sitting in your belly, waiting to be released.

When you are bloated or weighed down by what's sitting in your bowels, you can feel lethargic and uncomfortable, which makes it tough to feel energized and alert! So take 5 minutes in the morning and see if you can get rid of what's making you uncomfortable. You'll likely feel refreshed and as light as a feather! Sure, if you can't go, you don't need to sit there in frustration, but giving yourself 5 minutes to feel relaxed enough to try to use the bathroom can help you wake up faster and settle your stomach.

Sometimes it's hard to feel able to go when you're pressed for time, so set your alarm 5 minutes early. This way you will feel at ease and still make it out the door on time. Let your body do what it needs to be restored and carry on with normal body processes in a healthy, comfortable manner. Your energy levels will thank you!

START DINNER

Whether you work late hours or just want to unwind upon arriving home, it can be helpful to begin the process of preparing or cooking dinner early in the morning before heading out the door. The realization that you'll be more prepared for the day and evening ahead can make you feel more energized and eager to head out the door, and the act of chopping, storing, and washing different foods gets your body moving and activates the mind. Prepping your dinner now will save your time and energy later and give you that that much-needed mental and physical boost that will get you moving in the morning.

Are you making a stew in the slow cooker? You can place the ingredients in the slow cooker and set the timer for it to cook throughout the day. Once returning home, it'll be ready to eat—and you'll likely be starving as well!

Are you cooking a stir-fry and need to chop tons of vegetables for the dish? Take 5 minutes to chop up whatever you can in that period of time. You can then wrap the veggies or place them in a bowl to keep in the fridge until you get home.

PART 4

ENERGIZE YOUR AFTERNOON

TAKE THE STAIRS!

If you're in need of a quick boost of energy in the afternoon, getting your heart rate up with a burst of cardio will jolt the mind and body and improve focus for the remainder of the day. If you can't find time to make it to a workout class or the gym during your lunch break, just head to the stairwell for a 5-minute session! Here are a few exercises you can do to feel the burn and reset the body. You can choose one and repeat for 5 minutes, or you can try a couple of different ones.

Energizing Stair Exercises to Try

- **Do lunges.** You can do lunges on the stairwell by stepping up on every other step, to the point where you feel the extension in your legs and are working your glute muscles (in the buttocks) and thighs. You can lunge up and then either walk or run down the stairs.
- **Run up and down the stairs.** Seems pretty easy, but don't worry, you'll quickly get fatigued. Run up and down at your fastest pace to make it more of a sprint—you'll burn the highest number of possible calories.
- **Hop up the stairs and run back down.** You can either hop up on a single leg—which will be more of a challenge—or you can hop up each step with both feet. Run back down as fast as you can.

- **Run up and down the stairs with a weight.** You can stash a weight in your desk at work and take it with you to the stairwell. Make sure it's a weight you can hold as you run up and down. You can test it out at home first if you're concerned.

Exercising on the stairs can be done basically anywhere, so it's a great way to get your heart rate up and that energy boost when you can't make it to the gym or are short on time.

TAKE A BRISK WALK

If you're feeling run-down in the afternoon, forget that 5-minute coffee break and take a brisk walk outdoors! The fresh air will boost your energy levels and mood. And the moderately intense walk will improve blood circulation and awaken those tired muscles that have been stuck in an office chair for the last couple of hours.

What's more, you can benefit from seeing others outside, as research has shown that human contact can improve health and happiness. The visual stimulation will also help enhance your mental and physical state, as it will give you something new and interesting to observe. If you're walking in a new place, it'll further benefit the mind as it gives into its curious nature. You can take the walk solo or with a coworker. It's a matter of preference, but going outdoors with a coworker and someone to talk to and share the experience with could make this break more enjoyable. On a rainy day, just walk around the office or find a new indoor area to explore!

SPLASH COOL WATER ON YOUR FACE

Water has magical powers when it comes to refreshing the mind and body and making you more mentally alert. If you're feeling run-down midday, head to the bathroom and splash a bit of cool water on your face. It'll instantly reboot your system as it brings your body temperature down (whereas heat can make you weary and sluggish), so you can get back to your day without any fatigue weighing you down.

Water symbolizes rebirth, so think of a splash of water as a moment for rejuvenation. You can use your hands to wash your face, or you can use a wetted towel to dab cold water on your pulse points, cheeks, and forehead. The towel method might be less messy if you are concerned about splashing water on your clothing or smudging any foundation or mascara.

PRACTICE A POWER POSE

When you're feeling drained in the afternoon and need to improve confidence and energy, sit in a power pose position, which research has shown can instantly make you feel more self-assured, awake, and in control of your surroundings. And when it comes to owning your presence and invigorating all parts of the body and mind, the way you hold yourself and look outward to those around you directly impacts mood and positivity.

There are a few different ways to do a power pose, all with the same energy and mood benefits. Choose whichever position is most comfortable for you. You could feel fantastic in one position but not so great in another. Test them out to find one that works for you.

Try These Power Poses!

- Straighten your back and fix your posture so you're upright with your chest out. Your head should be straight or even slightly lifted, which can exude confidence. Let your shoulders widen and move backward, allowing your chest to expand and come forward. Take a deep breath. Inhale and exhale for a few minutes, and let the power take over your mind and body.
- Sit back in a chair with one leg bent and crossed over your other leg's knee. Let your arms relax on your armrest. This power pose will make you feel dominant and in charge—which is perfect for making some serious moves later in the day.

- Stand with your hands planted on the sides of your hips, with your back upright so you don't hunch over (which can make you feel weak and fatigued). Your head should be upright, looking straight ahead. This position will make you feel strong and in control of where you are and how you are handling yourself.

These simple confidence-boosting poses will make you feel energized and empowered, and they can be done anywhere, so enjoy!

INHALE ESSENTIAL OILS

Research has shown that essential oils, which are distilled oils often sourced from plants or other natural sources, can provide mental stimulation and possess properties that can balance the body and improve blood flow and circulation. When you find yourself low in energy midday, you might find that sniffing essential oils works well to reboot your physical and mental state. You'll want to take a few minutes to really practice inhaling and absorbing the aromas of the oils. Let them enter your nostrils and flow throughout your body—touching all parts from head to toe. A few suggestions of oils to try include these:

- Basil
- Cedarwood
- Cinnamon
- Eucalyptus
- Ginger
- Grapefruit
- Jasmine
- Juniper
- Lemon
- Lemongrass
- Orange
- Peppermint

- Spearmint
- Thyme

Carry these oils with you in a bag or keep them stashed in a drawer at the office, where you can access them whenever you need to. You can also store a few different scents to bring in some variety throughout the week. Test them all out, and see which oils work best for you in providing stimulation.

DRINK A GLASS OF COLD WATER

Research has shown that drinking cold water, as opposed to water at room temperature, will better energize the body, increase performance, and burn more calories—which makes ice water especially great when you're experiencing an afternoon slump. Besides the chill aspect, water will hydrate your body, and it's common to become fatigued, light-headed, and low in energy when your body and brain cells are lacking in water. Dehydration is also more common in the afternoon, especially if you've been eating a lot of sodium-rich foods—such as dressings, cottage cheese, nuts, or deli sandwiches—or sweating through basic movement during the day or potential work stress. As the body starts to lose fluids through perspiration and urination, it needs more water to feel restored and prevent fatigue. It makes sense: the body is about 60 percent water, so it needs to stay hydrated to function properly and have optimal performance, both physically and mentally.

Aim to drink about eight or more glasses a day, but if you feel tired during an afternoon slump, reach for a glass of cold water to see if you perk up. You'll probably feel more awake in a few minutes, and it'll help fill you up and make you less likely to crave sugar or processed foods later.

CHAT WITH A COWORKER

Studies have shown the energizing benefits of having a tight-knit social network, one made up of family, friends, coworkers, and even unexpected relationships found in unlikely places, such as the barista at your local coffee shop or the doorman in your office building! Being close to others creates a sense of vigor, which can permeate into all areas of your life. So if you're struggling with low energy in the afternoon, take a few moments to walk to another cubicle or floor and indulge in a nice chat with a coworker—she will probably be in need of one too!

You can talk about anything, depending on how intimate the relationship is. The topic can be simple, such as discussing the weather or an upcoming happy hour or event, or you can share details about family or hobbies. Either way, keep the conversation light and upbeat, as something too morose could negatively affect energy, depending on the circumstances. Keep it short, and then get back to whatever it was you were doing!

DO SQUATS

Get your legs loose and fight any kinks that may have been caused by sitting too long by standing up and doing a few rounds of squats! Squats are great for strengthening muscle and creating lean definition, and they increase blood flow and circulation, which can provide energy to different parts of the body—the mind included! Squat exercises will immediately boost your brain cells and keep them active, giving them the push you need to get through the remainder of your day. There are a few different types of squats you can do. Test them out to see what feels comfortable for you and doesn't put pressure on your knees.

Squats to Try!

- **Basic squat:** Simply stand straight with your legs spread not too wide—just a little past your shoulder width so you can easily squat down without causing strain to the joints. Stick your butt out as you go lower, with your back flat and not hunched over. Rounding your back could cause tension, which could set you up for injury. Sink down and feel the squat; then come up to standing. Repeat for a few rounds.

- **Jump squat:** Repeat the same squat form, but add in a plyometric move—an explosive exercise meant to spike your heart rate and create instant energy, such as a jump. After you sink into the squat, jump upward before returning to standing. Let your arms help propel you upward, and keep them loose.

- **Squat and pulse:** You can also go down into a squat and then pulse, with little "mini squats" within that squat position to further work those leg muscles. Pulse a few times before returning to standing, at which point you'll give your glutes a good squeeze before heading back down. The pulses will really work those lower body muscles.

- **Squat and half rise:** Squat down really deep and then come halfway up and hold for 5 to 10 seconds. Sink back down into the squat, and then return to standing. Repeat this exercise for a few rounds. The half raise and hold will require a lot of energy and focus to maintain a set position with a hold for a period of time.

Not only will squats increase blood flow and circulation in the legs for greater energy, but they'll also help tone your legs and build strength for more long-term benefits.

GRAB A HANDFUL OF NUTS

Nuts are a great snack to munch on in the afternoon, as they are high in key nutrients that will supply energy, protein, and good fats to keep you full and satisfied for the next few hours. These good fats include unsaturated fats and omega-3 fatty acids, which have been found to lower inflammation in the body and improve cognitive health, memory retention, and focus. In fact, several studies have demonstrated how beneficial omega-3s are in lowering the risk of dementia and Alzheimer's disease. Omega-3s are found in walnuts, while all other nuts have healthy unsaturated fats instead.

Beyond good fats, nuts also have protein and fiber to keep cravings at bay and squash hunger. Protein and fiber will improve your energy stores and will keep your energy levels elevated for a longer amount of time than sugary, processed foods or refined carbohydrates that are lacking in fiber. If you're looking for as much fiber as you can get, turn to pistachios, which have the largest amount of fiber per serving of all nuts.

Be sure to buy your nuts in the shell—the act of removing these shells will slow you down, so you'll fill up faster and be more mindful when eating. (Just don't eat the shell—it's not edible!) Mindfulness when eating will also improve energy and focus, and it can enhance your overall well-being. When you are aware of your surroundings, your appetite, and your current emotions, you're more likely to be mentally awake and focused on the present.

A few notable nuts to nibble on include these:

- Almonds
- Cashews
- Peanuts
- Pistachios
- Walnuts
- Pecans
- Macadamia nuts

Eat a handful of nuts with a string cheese or a piece of fruit. This will make for a well-rounded snack that's high in all the nutrients you need to power through until the evening. However, be mindful of portion sizes, as some nuts have larger recommended serving sizes than others. Look up suggestions before digging into the container carefree.

WRITE A HAIKU

If you're looking for a short activity that will stimulate the brain and help you think creatively, try writing a haiku! Haikus, a type of Japanese poetry, are easy and fun to write. They consist of three lines:

1. Line one has five syllables
2. Line two has seven syllables
3. Line three has five syllables

Your poem can be about anything you want—ideally, something related to your current mood and state of being. Look into your soul and pull something out. Whatever emotions you have, let them come out through words. Have some fun with it, and use your imagination. It's a nice break from whatever mundane project you have on your hands.

You can either share the haiku with others or keep it to yourself. You also can save all your haikus in a book, so you can keep a collection and access them whenever you'd like!

EAT SOME FRUIT!

If you're looking for an increase in energy, a piece of fruit can do the trick. Fruit is naturally high in sugar, meaning it will increase your blood glucose levels. But as fruit is natural and high in fiber, it won't cause a spike that could lead to a crash like sugary processed foods could do. The natural sugar will fight fatigue and any light-headedness you might be experiencing during the afternoon slump, and it's easy to carry a piece of fruit with you during the day, whether whole to munch on or as part of a fruit salad that's stored in the fridge. Plus, fruit is healthy—it's high in antioxidants to better your heart health and combat aging, and it's a great way to satisfy a sweet tooth without eating junk food. Here are a few suggestions for a fruity snack that'll energize you when your energy stores run low.

Energy-Boosting Fruits to Try

- Grab an apple and spread some nut butter on top. The combination of fruit and nut butter provides complex carbohydrates and fiber, which supplies immediate but long-lasting energy, and the nut butter offers healthy fats and protein to improve the absorption of nutrients and keep you full.
- For instant energy, nosh on fruit with cheese for both protein and fast-acting carbs. Eat a pear or an orange with a string cheese (or a few cubes of cheese). The cheese will go nicely with

fruit and provides protein to make the fruit feel more like a well-rounded snack. Tarter fruits, like apples, cranberries, or grapes, might taste great with nuttier or more versatile cheeses, such as Gouda, Cheddar, or mozzarella, while sweeter fruits, like berries or figs, could be better with ricotta, goat, or Brie. However, it's up to your taste buds, so experiment with different combinations.

- Eat dried fruit with yogurt. Top yogurt with some raisins, apricots, or figs, but be careful with portion control, as dried fruit can be extremely high in sugar and calories per serving. It's not the same as fresh fruit! If you're concerned, throw berries into Greek yogurt instead.

Just be sure to keep portion control in check—a serving or two of fruit for a snack is enough, and pairing the fruit with the protein will make sure that the energy from the fruit is sustained for the next few hours.

PINCH YOURSELF

When you feel lethargic or stressed out, as if you're losing the stamina to carry on with a pressing assignment at hand, pinch yourself on your arm or leg—wherever there's a bit of skin to pull in a spot that won't cause pain. That small discomfort will instantly shock you, waking up your brain and body and bringing you back to an aware and awake state. Ouch—right? Well, not really. As long as you're gentle and you know it's coming, that pinch won't be as painful as you think.

Make a goal to pinch yourself when you start to look tired or have hit the dreaded "tired hour" most people have become accustomed to in the afternoon. Pinch your arm or back—somewhere that's fleshy enough that it won't hurt. And do it lightly; it'll still be effective! If you have trouble remembering, you can also set an alarm on your phone to go off every half hour—if you find yourself getting tired once the alarm rings, then pinch away!

WASH YOUR HANDS

Much like cold water on your face and body can energize you, so can lathering your hands in soap and cool water! It'll feel great on your fingers, which may have gone a tad numb from typing on a keyboard or dialing numbers on a phone all day. Plus, it gets your legs moving as you're forced to head toward the bathroom and the sink. Simply getting up and walking a short distance alone will energize you, and the cool water will reboot your mind and body.

Cold water will also bring your body temperature down. Studies have shown that a lower body temperature can improve thinking and performance, while hotter temperatures can make you drowsy and dizzy at times. Take a few minutes to really lather those hands, let the cool water seep into your skin, and start to feel that energy boost creep in!

HOLD YOUR BREATH

Holding your breath is hard to do and requires concentration, which can immediately boost brainpower and energy levels. Be careful when doing this activity, though! You need to know when to let the air out in order to keep your body safe and get the real benefits. You don't want to feel too uncomfortable, feel any pain, or have difficulty breathing.

Listen to how your body feels. Hold your breath until you can't hold it anymore, then wait a minute or two to breathe normally and let the air energize your body. Then you can repeat this activity again until you reach a total time of 5 minutes. Focus on the breath, whether you're holding it in or breathing normally. Breath work and mindfulness will increase awareness and wakefulness, leading to higher energy stores.

STRETCH YOUR ANKLES

If you've been sitting down for a few hours, your ankles can become stiff, tired, and in need of a burst of energy. When you do stand up, it could take a while to ease into the movement unless you've taken some walking breaks during the day. To improve circulation in your ankles, which can then create a flow of energy that can circulate throughout your entire body, try a few ankle exercises that will loosen up the area and relieve any tension. You can stick with one stretch and repeat it a few times, or you can try them all for the full 5 minutes of work.

Some Ankle Stretches to Try

- Twist your ankles in and out, moving to and from each side. Sit on the ground with your legs extended out in front of you, move your right ankle inward toward the other leg and foot as far as you can go and then outward with the same extension. Then do this on the other leg.
- Draw out the letters of the alphabet with your big toe. Those ABCs will come in handy to increase flexibility and mobility in the ankles and to get rid of any pooled blood that could be draining energy in other areas of the body. Use your toe to simply go through each letter, tracing it on the ground.
- Sit in a chair and push your ankle to one side and hold, with toes pointed on the ground. Let your butt and hip move to the side

you're leaning toward with your ankle. Start with the right foot. Gently shift your weight in the ankle toward the right side and hold for a few seconds. Return back to neutral and repeat in the left direction. Once finished, repeat this exercise on the left foot. You can do a few rounds, alternating between feet.

- Rock up and down, shifting weight between the toes and heels. Think of it as bouncing up and down but with a controlled motion, switching between being on your tiptoes to flat on the ground. While you're energizing your whole foot, you're really getting into those tight ankles and bringing back flexibility and range of motion.

These ankle exercises are sure to improve circulation, preventing any stagnation of blood that can drain you of energy throughout the body. Do these exercises for 5 minutes total.

LOOK UP A RESTAURANT MENU

If you start to feel your energy levels dipping in the afternoon, take a moment to look up a new restaurant's menu. It's a good distraction and gives you something to look forward to trying in the future. Plus, nothing is quite as energizing—to the mind *and* belly—as thinking about food. And when there's a visual aspect, such as a menu or gallery of photos, it can be even more stimulating! You can find a restaurant you've heard of, ask a coworker for a restaurant recommendation, or just do a *Google* search for your favorite food and a location to see what pops up.

Studies show that food can have a positive effect on the brain and mood, and eating food is often associated with increased happiness, especially when you're in a social environment. The menu items, images, and descriptions will make your mouth water and get your brain excited—and you'll probably want to book a reservation shortly after.

TEXT A FRIEND

Connecting with a friend or striking up a conversation that's light and enjoyable can immediately provide energy and a more positive outlook. When you're at work or going about your typical Sunday, you're often stuck doing the same mundane tasks—which of course must be taken care of, but that's why little 5-minute breaks are definitely necessary. Whether you're getting through emails or grocery shopping for the week, taking a 5-minute break can be a pleasant distraction. After all, there's only so much time and effort the brain can spend on a given area at once, so picking up your phone and texting a friend will distract the mind and give it something new to focus on.

Texting is really easy, as it takes only a few seconds and you're still able to dive into a longer conversation if you choose to. However, if you prefer a visual aspect to your conversation, try videochatting via a service like *Skype* or *FaceTime*. Just be warned—if your buddy is at work and not on a lunch break, don't be surprised if he doesn't pick up.

CLEAN YOUR GLASSES

When there's fogginess in your line of vision, there's going to be fogginess in your mind as well. Not seeing clearly can cause fatigue and sleepy, droopy eyes, which aren't so great for getting you through that afternoon slump. Fortunately, seeing clearly can boost energy and maintain higher levels, since it will keep you awake and able to recognize and appreciate visual stimuli.

So if you're wearing dirty glasses and starting to zone out, take 5 minutes to clean them with a cloth that can protect the lens and wipe away any gunk.

Here's how to properly clean your glasses, because *no*, it's not enough to just wipe them on your shirt!

How to Clean Your Glasses

- Wash your hands—you don't want to clean your lenses with dirty hands. You're trying to get rid of the germs!
- Rinse your glasses in the sink with warm water. Wet both sides of the lenses.
- Use a drop of lotion-free dish soap to gently lather your lenses with your fingertips.
- Use a cotton swab to wash the nose pads and tough-to-reach areas.
- Wash your glasses under warm water again to get rid of the dish soap. Then dry them with a microfiber cloth, making

circular motions with your fingers to clean each lens and to wipe the nose pad.

This stands true for everyday glasses, reading glasses, or even sunglasses!

SCRATCH YOUR BACK

The sensation of a scratch is a major wake-up call—it's slightly aggressive and provides adequate pressure to jolt the mind and trigger a reaction. So if you're feeling tired midafternoon, give your back a scratch to get those energy levels soaring!

Scratch in a place that's accessible, such as the upper back by the neck and shoulder blades or on the sides of the low back. You don't want to strain yourself trying to reach the middle of the back and other unreachable areas. This could actually cause you to pull something, which could be dangerous, as back pain is a pretty serious injury that requires specific treatment and care. Also, be careful not to scratch too hard, especially if you have sharp nails. You don't want to leave a red mark! Instead, scratch hard enough to notice the force but light enough so it can be relaxing as well.

If you can't do it yourself, you can also always buy a wooden back scratcher to really hit those hard-to-reach spots.

EAT SOMETHING SALTY

Feeling tired? Your afternoon energy loss could be from a loss of electrolytes such as potassium, magnesium, and calcium, which are lost through sweat, excretion, and even overconsumption of water. (Yes, you can actually drink too many fluids, so be mindful as to how thirsty your body feels throughout the day. This is pretty rare, though, so don't be too concerned!) When you need to restore depleted electrolytes, grabbing a snack with a bit of salt (like the ones on the following list) can help perk you up and boost those energy levels!

Salty Snacks to Try

- **Cottage cheese:** You better believe it—cottage cheese is surprisingly high in sodium, despite its other health benefits and nutritional value. For instance, a serving can have between 400 milligrams and 800 milligrams of sodium. Still, a cup of cottage cheese with fresh fruit could be the pick-me-up you're looking for!
- **Nuts:** A handful of salted nuts will boost brainpower, as studies have shown the cognitive benefits of eating nuts as a high-protein, magnesium-rich snack. Nuts are also excellent sources of healthy fats, which reduce inflammation in the brain and body to help you focus and feel more energized.
- **Roasted legumes:** Roasted beans and legumes, such as chickpeas, broad beans, and edamame, are great options for filling,

portable snacks during the day that offer enough sodium. That bit of saltiness, paired with a seasoning of your choice, will make you more alert. Try adding spices like wasabi, curry, garlic, onion, and cayenne—the heat will further boost your brain and metabolism, leading to greater, steadier energy levels.

You don't want to eat too much salt, though, as salty foods in excess can increase the risk of heart disease, high blood pressure and cholesterol, stroke, and diabetes. Salt is also a major bloater, leading to inflammation and more water retention, which can make you puffy and swollen. So eat these foods, but stay within the correct serving size when you go this route.

STRETCH YOUR BACK

The back holds on to so much tension, and it's easy to get a backache when you're not moving around a lot. Unfortunately, since your back affects your body's alignment and your posture, back pain can throw your whole body off. The best way to prevent back pain is to stretch it in the afternoon when you're especially prone to cramping up. In just 5 minutes, you'll keep your back strong and have more stable energy levels. You can either stick with one stretch and repeat it a few times to reach those 5 minutes, or you can try them all for the full 5 minutes of work.

Some Back Stretches to Try

- Stand and place your hands, palms spread wide, on your lower back, right above your hips. Place them firmly with your fingernails pointing down toward the floor. Then lift your back and spine upward, pressing your shoulders down. You'll feel a great stretch in the back, opening up any tight muscles and getting in a full breath too.
- Stand and clasp your hands together behind your back. Lift your torso up to correct your posture and add height, standing tall and proud. Push your arms and hands down toward the floor to feel that stretch. Then raise your clasped arms over your head, with the arms along the ears. Lift up with your torso and lean toward the right side, with straight arms clasped overhead and tilting to the right as well. Repeat this on the left side.

- Go on all fours and curl your back so it's moving upward, with your head loose and hanging below. Ease any tension in the neck by keeping it loose as well. Hold for a few seconds. Return to neutral and then arch the back so your head is straight and you're looking directly ahead. Alternate a few times. This exercise is very calming, so it will help center the mind and balance the body too.

These back exercises will create more energy and blood flow in the body and alleviate stress.

OPEN UP YOUR HIPS

The hips can get incredibly tight, and they actually affect more areas than you think. Bad back or posture? You might actually have excess tension in your hips, which is causing strain on the back instead. So while doing back exercises will help, you really need to work those hips as well to get to the root of the problem. Because hip health can influence energy levels and body aches (pain and soreness in the muscles and joints can lead to low energy and fatigue), spending 5 minutes to loosen up the trouble spots and open up those hips will energize all parts of the body. Here are a few exercises to keep in mind. You can either stick with one stretch and repeat it a few times to reach the 5-minute mark, or you can try them all for the full 5 minutes of work.

Some Hip Stretches to Try

- Hold on to a bar or doorknob for stability, and lift your right leg up in front of you, holding your balance. Bend the right leg and place the ankle over the left knee, letting it rest there. Then sink down, letting the stretch open up the hips and improve the range of motion and flexibility. Hold for a minute, and then stand up and release. Repeat on the left side, and then repeat once more on each side.
- Spread your legs wide and sink down in the middle, as if you're doing a squat. Rest your arms on your knees and sink deeper.

Shift from side to side. If you can, try to touch your hands to the ground without bending your back.

- Go into a runner's lunge. You can start in the same form as the preceding exercise, but then turn your body to the right and lower into a lunge that's on the ground. Your right foot will be at 90 degrees and upright, while the left leg will be extended back behind you. Move gently forward to add more pressure and loosen up the hips even deeper. Repeat on the left side.

The hips can hold so much tension, which can zap energy, so eliminating stress can help you stay energized and mobile.

TAKE A CALL WHILE PACING

Studies have shown that fidgeting can improve both energy levels and cognitive function, so instead of taking a work call in your chair, jump on up and start pacing! This is a form of functional fidgeting that's bound to get you mobile and awake. Plus, the movement itself will speed circulation and encourage healthy blood flow, which will travel throughout the body and brain to provide fresh energy stores.

If you're at work and think you'll distract your coworkers, take the call by the bathroom or outside. Choose the latter option if it's available to you. The fresh air and nature will make you more aware of your surroundings and offer fresh oxygen to the lungs for more energy and wakefulness.

No work call required? Take a personal call instead! This 5-minute break will be even more pleasurable. Plus, keeping it short won't really take you away from work (it's as though you went to the bathroom or filled a water bottle!)—it'll refresh you and reboot your brain, helping you be more productive afterward.

ROTATE YOUR WRISTS

You may be surprised to hear that circling and even cracking your wrists can make you more energized. Beyond the mere aspect of sound, as the cracking noise can be energizing on its own, it's a way to build movement in the body, which can create energy throughout the limbs and in the joints and muscles. Joints can become stiff and achy, and when that happens, energy can dip as the body gets tired and sore. It's super easy to circle or crack your wrists too, as you don't need equipment and you can do it right in your chair. Plus, while it does make a sound (if it cracks), it's not a loud noise, so it won't disturb your neighbors. Circle your wrists in the right direction and then circle in the left direction. Alternate for a few minutes. You can also pull your palms back gently to flex the hands, which will also loosen the wrists, in between circles.

PAT YOURSELF ON THE BACK

Sometimes you need to just give yourself a pat on the back—it's that special reassurance that everything's going to be okay. When you take a few moments to relish in human touch, you're boosting feel-good hormones, like oxytocin (the love hormone), that will give you a major lift in energy and mood. It's like you're giving yourself a physical pep talk, and this recognition of acceptance and love will give you renewed energy and confidence to go about your day. Pat with a little bit of pressure (not too much where you're in pain!), as that force will further wake you up.

And since you're the one giving yourself a bit of love, you're increasing your self-worth and confidence, which will make you more prone to feelings of vigor, excitement, and empowerment on a regular basis. When doing something that feels daring and aligned with how you value yourself and your abilities, it can motivate you to use that energy to make even more radical changes and live life to the fullest.

GIVE YOURSELF A MASSAGE

Similar to the idea of a pat on the back, a massage will provide energy and increase blood flow and circulation throughout the body. You can massage any area you like. If your shoulders and neck are tense, work your hands through those knots and release the tension. When there's built-up stress in your muscles, it can cause fatigue and soreness, which will deplete energy levels. Don't place too much pressure where you're in pain—as this can actually damage those muscles and create more tension—but be sure to give enough pressure so you can really feel the area loosen.

If you don't want to work those areas, you can give yourself a foot massage, a temple rub, or even a massage on the thighs simply by stroking and squeezing your legs while sitting in a chair. It'll feel good to reboot the body, and the massage itself helps the body and mind wake up through this small act of force!

PAT SOMEONE ELSE ON THE SHOULDER

Do a good deed for a friend and give someone's shoulder some love and care. When you show gratitude and compassion for others, it will energize the mind and body and make you feel more alive and connected to your surrounding network. Plus, the aspect of human touch stimulates energy, and as you're the one giving a pat or light massage to someone else, your hands are put to work as well. Doing something physical will encourage energy production and focus, and something so small as a light touch will still do the trick. You can pat a friend or family member when you're looking for a personal boost in energy, or you can ask your recipient in advance for a time that might be appropriate. (You don't want to interrupt a friend on a phone call or on a date to give a pat on the shoulder, right?) Use your best judgment.

PRACTICE KANBAN

You might be scratching your head, but this energy hack is well worth the exploration. Kanban is a technique that boosts productivity and can increase energy. It improves organization and time management, thus improving efficiency. If your stamina is draining and you need that energy boost to be more productive, kanban can help you recharge.

How to Do Kanban

1. Divide your to-dos into separate sections: "ready," "doing," and "done." These three categories will help separate tasks into their given areas, so you can better clear your head, feel focused, and gain control of your to-do list. For example, let's say you have "write a proposal for a client" on your calendar. It'll be under the "ready" section once you've gathered your materials and can begin. Then, it'll get moved to "doing" while you're in the process of writing it up. Once it's completed and emailed to the client, you can move it to "done," where it will remain as you let it leave your mind and move on to the next task that's waiting in the "ready" category. The same goes for nonwork tasks—if you're planning a birthday party, go through each step until the process is complete and all that's left is to wait for the happy occasion to arrive.

2. As you keep going through your list and sorting tasks into designated categories, you'll likely feel accomplished, as though a

weight has been lifted. Check in and tell yourself how successful you are—let yourself feel the pride and that energy boost that comes with filling the "done" category on your list in order to get even more work done.

3. Consider how much time something has spent in each category. For instance, if you have a "ready" item that has been sitting there for a while, consider why it's been a point of procrastination. What's stopping you? Why does it not energize you? Think of a way to get more motivated to begin the task. This can be helpful in making sure you can garner enough energy in times when it's naturally low.

By staying organized and tracking accomplishments each step of the way, you're able to stay energized and motivated until the very end.

BITE YOUR TONGUE

If you're dealing with an energy lull, a slight bite of your tongue can add just the right amount of pressure to wake you up and get you back to reality. Any sort of pressure will provide awareness, drawing your attention to the present moment and creating focused energy. When you concentrate on a specific action, you're immediately increasing energy levels and clearing your mind for whatever's next on your to-do list.

Take a small bite into the tip of your tongue. Press down gently with your teeth for a nibble and hold it there. You can even do small nibbles, if you prefer. If the tongue feels too sensitive, you can bite the side of your gums instead. However, be careful not to cause irritation to the area. Any trauma to the mouth could result in issues such as cysts, cold sores, canker sores, and other types of inflammation. These can become painful and might need further treatment in order to heal.

SQUEEZE A STRESS BALL

There's a reason people keep stress balls on their desks—they are great for improving energy levels and getting out some stress! Anxiety can drain energy and make you lose motivation and stamina, so a few squeezes of a stress ball can go a long way in getting your aggression out in a healthy manner and helping you feel invigorated once again.

Keep a stress ball at your desk so you can access it when you're starting to get burned out midday. While you're squeezing, think about whatever it is that's making you tense. Then acknowledge its power and let your emotions come out. Let the stress ball help remove them from your mind. Once you've spent a minute using the ball on that one thought, let it go and move on to the next. When you're done, you'll be in a much better mindset and will feel eager to get back to work with a positive, energetic attitude.

BOB YOUR HEAD TO A SONG

The combination of a piece of music's beats and lyrics can really resonate with the mind, body, and soul. And music can play a huge part in making you feel energized and awake—especially when you keep your head moving along with the beat!

Often the afternoon slump can zap energy, and you forget the intentions you had set out earlier in the day. A solution? Pick a song that makes you feel invigorated and excited to make great things happen that day. Let yourself feel the rhythm and go with the flow. Bobbing your head will further boost energy in your mind and help you relate better to the sound and lyrics. You'll be present in that given moment and regain motivation to get back to the daily grind. Connecting to music will help you be more aware of your surroundings, and the bobbing motion will wake the body up and get your blood flowing.

WHISTLE!

Whistling isn't easy, and while some people are naturals, others need to practice to get a tune going. (And some may never really get it at all!) Whether you can whistle a tune perfectly or you're just trying to get the hang of it, whistling requires energy and attention in order to make it work. By focusing your mind and body on the action (whistling requires both), you'll improve your cognitive function and boost those energy levels!

Give yourself a few minutes to try to learn how to whistle, or spend some time whistling to different tunes. You can even make up your own jingle—the extra aspect of creativity will further enhance energy levels and get your brain working. If you can whistle and find a song you like, you'll also become more energized from the musical and sentimental aspects of whatever you're whistling.

STICK YOUR HEAD OUT THE WINDOW

Let that fresh air rejuvenate you and provide a new stream of energy to brighten your day and get your brain and body revved up. Studies have shown that nature and fresh air can instantly provide energy and a lift in mood, so if you can't make it outside for a brisk walk, a coffee break, or a seat on a bench to relax, simply opening the window and sticking your head outdoors can still provide long-lasting benefits!

This will immediately get rid of fatigue, especially if there's a bit of a breeze or chill in the air—cooler temperatures can make you more awake. If it's too cold for you, simply crack the window and don't stick your head out fully. Do whatever is comfortable for you, and enjoy the energy boost!

JUMP ROPE

A jump rope is easy to store in a desk or carry in your bag, and it's a great way to get an instant kick of energy for the mind and body. Getting regular exercise will improve cognitive function, memory retention, productivity levels, and the ability to think creatively and outside the box. In fact, studies show that you might even get your most brilliant ideas and help retain important information while working out. As a bonus, jumping rope burns about 10 calories per minute, so if you go for 5 whole minutes, you'll get a total of 50 calories shaved off that afternoon lunch. Not so bad, right?

Keep a jump rope on hand and aim to do 5 minutes of work at least once a day when energy is low. If you like it, you can even incorporate 5-minute bursts into your daily schedule by spacing them out every hour or so.

WEAR RED!

Studies have shown that the color red can make you feel more energized and confident since it's a color of authority, dominance, and passion. Consider putting on a red jacket or changing into a fresh pair of red socks to let the color take its effect. If you're a woman, you can also opt for a nice shade of red lipstick, going bright or deep, depending on your facial hues and preferences.

Lipstick is super easy to carry around with you, as it fits right in a makeup bag or clutch. You can also store it in a desk drawer. So swipe on a layer of red lipstick after lunch, and check your appearance in a mirror. Let the color energize and empower you. If you need a little push, recite a positive mantra while staring at your reflection to really own the moment, then get out there and take on your to-do list! For more information on the benefits of positive self-talk, look to "Recite Powerful Words" and "Practice Positive Affirmation," both in Part 2.

MAKE A YES/MEH LIST

There are bound to be a few tasks that are sucking your energy, and if you're given the choice to dismiss them, do so! This will allow you to focus your attention on things that uplift you and make you feel awake and invigorated instead. Here's what to do:

1. Get a pen and paper or open your laptop to start a list of items or tasks that are enhancing or zapping your energy stores. Put the items that enhance your energy stores in a "yes" column and the ones that drain your energy or weigh on your mind in a "meh" column.

2. Look at the items that are on your "meh" list. Maybe it contains things like the need to go grocery shopping and cook dinner after work. Consider whether you should forgo them and create a "yes" instead. Here, a "yes" might be ordering in or going out to dinner as a family instead and scheduling a grocery store trip for the next day. Or you could get delivery from the store, depending on the availability of this service in your area. For instance, Whole Foods has partnered with Instacart so you can often order items from the store straight to your home.

3. In addition to swapping "meh" items for more "yes" items, consider items that are natural "yes" aspects of your life already and look to them to provide energy. For instance, does speaking to your child

or spouse on the phone during the day bring you energy? Does it instantly revitalize you and make you feel connected and loved? Then grab your phone and call, videochat, or send a text message! Doing so will make you feel refreshed and alive, and it'll get your head back into a positive state.

4. Keep track of these "yes" items, and use them for 5-minute energy hacks elsewhere. Honor them, and realize how influential they can be. Keep swapping "meh" tasks for "yes" ones, and add them to the ever-growing list.

That said, if a "meh" item is work related and essential to your job, there's no way to get around it; however, incorporating actions that might make the task easier, such as listening to music while doing it, could help.

DO A WALL SIT

Take a moment to work those glutes and thighs—a wall squat requires focus and energy, and the time you take to perform the exercise will improve energy stores and get your brain and body working again. Plus, assuming you've been sitting in a chair for a chunk of the day, it'll be an excuse to get blood flowing and increase circulation throughout your limbs. The heat in your muscles from the wall sit will also create heat in the body, which in turn produces more energy too. Here's what to do:

1. Keep your weight in your thighs and glutes as you sink into a squat down to the halfway point of a wall. Make sure your knees are bent in front of you and your back is flat against the wall. Sit for 60 seconds. Then get up and rest for 60 seconds. Repeat. Do this exercise, alternating time, for 5 minutes if you can. You'll definitely get the energizing benefits, along with the strengthening perks that'll improve muscle gains and endurance.

2. Another option is to let someone else in on the fun! You can do partner wall sits by using each other's backs as a replacement for the wall and lowering down into a squat together. Make sure you're even, where you're at the same height above ground for better balance. Do the same exercise with 60 seconds on and off for a total of 5 minutes. This variation requires another level of focus, which further improves energy—you're not only working

your own legs and going at an intensity that works for you, but you're also influencing another person's body and activity level. It requires more attention to detail to use another person's body weight as equipment and work together as a team.

No matter which option you choose, you'll be feeling more energized in no time!

PART 5
ENERGIZE YOUR EVENING

DANCE WHEN MAKING DINNER

As you're chopping veggies and waiting for your chicken to cook, turn on some music and dance around the kitchen. The music and dancing will bring energy, making cooking seem less like a chore and more like a fun way to unwind after a long day. In fact, cooking can actually be quite meditative, helping to energize and focus the mind and body. Plus, the act of cooking can become ingrained as an automatic behavior—one that doesn't really require much thinking once you know what to do and have a repertoire of go-to recipes. This makes it a great way to zone out so you can focus on livening up the moment. For even more energy, ask your spouse or children to join in on the fun! You can even make up a dinner dance with them as a way to act out different motions, such as stirring soup or sprinkling seasonings.

EAT A HEALTHY MEAL

After a long day, you may find yourself starving and tired, and finding the right kind of fuel will immediately replenish depleted energy levels. If you're eating dinner, have something that contains a balance of healthy fats, protein, and complex carbohydrates. This combination of different nutrients will optimize energy and provide staying power to keep energy levels stable and prevent a carb crash later. If you're having just an early evening snack, halve the portions or stick to something smaller, such as nuts and a piece of fruit or a slice of whole-wheat bread with avocado.

There are a few different things you can eat that will fill you up and provide energy without leading to a crash, as sugary and processed foods would. (That's why you shouldn't *really* down a double bacon cheeseburger or a huge bowl of pasta with Alfredo sauce for dinner.) Here are a few delicious options to eat for dinner.

Energizing Dinner Dishes

- A 6-ounce piece of chicken breast or fish filet, such as salmon, halibut, or tilapia, along with a side of starch, such as brown rice or quinoa, and a heavy heaping of vegetables. Don't drench your veggies in butter or creamy sauces, though—use a healthy oil, such as olive oil or avocado oil, or a nonstick spray to cook. Or steam them!

- Four ounces of red meat, half of a baked sweet potato, and lots and lots of veggies! Try Brussels sprouts or asparagus to get some greens in. You can also add a light salad or soup. Keep the soup broth-based, rather than cream-based; a light, low-calorie soup will fill your belly and prevent overeating, while heavy soups will weigh you down and add calories. As for the salad, use only a tad of dressing (a forkful spread throughout) or a drizzle of olive oil, and include healthy ingredients rather than unhealthy, processed ones, such as bacon bits, dried cranberries, or croutons.

By eating something nutritious for dinner, you'll be able to have enough energy to enjoy your evening—whether that's family fun night or a movie.

CLEAN SOMETHING IN YOUR HOME

Seems ironic, but a great way to energize yourself at the end of the day is to clean! Studies show that when your space is clean and free of germs, you're likely to feel more invigorated, focused, and in control of your surroundings. When you're amid a mess, it can make you feel like a mess, which sucks energy and weighs you down.

It's not just the cleaning mindset that brings clarity and alertness, though. It's also about the movement itself since you're working with your arms, hands, and legs to clean up around the house. What's more, scented cleaning products or solutions will stimulate the senses, leading to even greater energy levels. A bonus? A lemon scent or something that contains citrus will make you even more awake, as studies have shown that the smell of citrus can provide a lift in energy and mood.

Of course, you can clean for however long you like, but you really just need 5 minutes to get a lot accomplished and a boost in energy. So after a long day, fight fatigue by cleaning something! Scrub your counter, a dirty dish, or even the toilet (just squirt some solution in and you'll still feel the perks—how easy is that?)! If you're concerned about finding enough to clean, think outside the box. You can wipe down the mirrors, dust under the bed, or even just change the sheets on the bed, which actually requires quite of a bit of manual labor and will surely give you that exercise boost.

MAKE TIME FOR SEX

When you're having sex, you're certainly getting those energy levels up. Your heart rate increases, feel-good hormones are released, and you're getting a sweat on—all of which can make you super alert and energized. Studies have expressed the many benefits of regularly having sex in terms of increased energy and happiness levels. Plus, it allows you to bond with your partner, thanks to the hormone oxytocin (the love hormone)! And simple intimacy and touch make you feel more invigorated overall. There's just too much energy-boosting goodness in sex to feel tired!

You can have sex either with your partner or alone. So if your partner is busy working, traveling, or out to dinner with friends, just close the bedroom door and give yourself some much-needed pleasure. It's totally okay and actually encouraged, as studies have shown that people who have sex (and orgasms) live longer and have more energy.

If you want to have sex with your partner but struggle to find the time, *make* the time. Between work, kids, chores, errands, friends, exercise, and other life matters to juggle each day, it can be hard to squeeze in sex. However, treat it as an appointment. Put it on the calendar. If it's more about setting the mood, bring out the candles, music, toys, Egyptian cotton sheets, or whatever else you might need to make the bedroom intimate and playful. You can even try having sex in different places if you're stuck in a rut. Draw a warm bath with bubbles and a bottle of wine. Or try having sex on the couch when the kids are asleep. Shake things up and step outside your comfort zone! You can try role-playing, toys, new lingerie—anything that'll bring novelty and adventure, which will add an extra bit of stimulation too.

PREP FOR TOMORROW

Nothing can make you more tired than thinking about what a stressful day you have ahead of you come morning. So take a few minutes once you're home in the evening to plan out the following day, jotting down everything you need to accomplish and providing steps for how best to find success and manage your time. Making a list is a great way to improve energy, as it gets you thinking in a productive manner. Knowing that you have a set list of things to do and a clear direction in mind for the following day will help you feel less stressed, so you can enjoy your current evening with newfound energy.

If you need to prioritize what you need to get done, write that down. If there's a morning errand you need to do in order to prepare for something later in the day, take note of that as well, and consider whether you might need to shift things around in the a.m., take your breakfast to go, or set the alarm earlier. Soon you'll have the energy to really enjoy your evening, knowing that you'll have a plan set for the next day.

DINE WITH GOOD COMPANY

When it comes to dinner, you can eat alone, but you probably won't feel as energized as you would with some good company and stimulating conversation. It could be a home-cooked meal with your family, an intimate date night with your spouse, or a girls' or guys' night out with the buds. Even dining out with a client or coworkers can provide energy, since you're out in a social environment with high energy, interesting dialogue, and many smiling faces that further promote lightheartedness and fun.

Let yourself have some time to eat and enjoy the company. There's no need to rush dinner and scarf down your food (which isn't so great for digestion and the metabolism anyway). After a busy day, you deserve the energy boost and downtime to feel rejuvenated. That way, you'll be motivated to get up and do it all again tomorrow!

WATCH YOUR FAVORITE TV SHOW

Sure, watching too much TV can drain energy and make you less productive (especially if you're watching clips at the office or putting off work to watch a show you enjoy), but as long as you're keeping your viewing time to a maximum of an hour or two a day, it's actually a great way to feel energized and restored!

Your favorite TV shows bring humor, love, romance, drama, and thrilling, mysterious stories that can grasp your attention and boost your mind and thoughts, creating various stimulating responses within the body. Just think about a scary show or movie—all that yelling and anticipation will get your mind racing, your heart rate up, and your body clenched all in one. Find something that makes you feel alive and happy, and let all the emotions that arise make you feel energized and wide, wide awake. However, turn the TV off at least 30 minutes before bed to unwind and get sleepy, or else you might be up for a while.

INDULGE IN DARK CHOCOLATE!

If you're getting home from a long day and feeling low on stamina, pop a square or two of dark chocolate for a burst in energy! Studies have shown that dark chocolate has caffeine, which provides a kick of energy and makes you more alert. It also contains antioxidants, which promote brain health and cognitive function, keeping you mentally aware.

However, make sure you're indulging only in dark chocolate, since milk and white chocolates don't have the same energizing benefits or antioxidants that can benefit the body. In fact, chowing down on a milk chocolate candy bar or a cookie with white chocolate chunks won't do you any favors—instead you'll get a sugar high and subsequent crash shortly after. So pick something dark (the darker, the better, in terms of antioxidants, purity, and energy-boosting qualities), but limit yourself to a moderate portion, which might be a square or two, depending on the bar. You can also go by the serving size listed on a chocolate bar or halve it, depending on how caloric of a treat you're looking for. Going overboard might actually make you sluggish from excess sugar and fat, and it can lead to unwanted weight gain over time.

USE A FOAM ROLLER

A foam roller can work wonders on tired, sore muscles! What's a foam roller? It's a piece of equipment that acts as a massager for the body. You can roll it on several areas of your body to get rid of knots and break up tension in your muscles. You can buy your own online; however, since it's highly encouraged post-workout, most gyms have foam rollers as well.

Even if you don't have tight muscles or trigger points on your legs and feet, taking a few minutes to use a foam roller will provide more energy and increase blood flow and circulation throughout the limbs, which also makes your body more agile. What's more, if you choose to use a foam roller each night, regardless of a workout or not, you'll help prevent chronic soreness, fatigue, and injury that can happen from workouts or just daily tasks.

Feeling tight and sluggish in your lower body especially can make you "drag" yourself along, which makes it challenging to maintain enough energy come evening, when all you want to do is plop down on the couch. So go over all the areas in your lower body—glutes, hamstrings, quads, calves—with the foam roller, and use a foam roller ball or tennis ball for your heels and feet. However, don't foam roll your back or IT band (a group of connective tissues along the outer thighbone and knees). These can be tricky areas to massage, and you don't want to do any damage.

WASH YOUR FACE!

When you get home at night, take 5 minutes to clean that sweat, oil, or makeup off your skin! Taking just 5 minutes to wash your face can boost your energy levels, since the water perks you up and the smell of the product you're using can stimulate your senses. Plus, that fresh, clean feeling you have from getting rid of any debris left over from the day goes a long way toward a sense of renewal.

You can either hop in the shower, as the warm or slightly cool water will further provide energy (as explained in the "Embrace the Water" entry in Part 1), or you can just go to the sink and give your face a wash. Cleaning your skin will help it stay fresh, acne-free, and glowing, and it'll also slow the signs of aging that come with, well, age, the use of various products, or environmental damage. And you don't want to sleep with a face that's dirty or covered in concealer!

If you're looking for a great skincare regimen, you can ask any skin expert at a department store or your dermatologist for recommendations on products and positive habits. Finding something that works for your complexion is key, and it should also be easy for you to use so you stick with it consistently.

CROSS OFF YOUR TO-DO LIST

When you get home but still have things left to take care of, you'll likely feel drained. It's like the day has ended but your workload and stress haven't. *Ugh*. As a solution, keep a to-do list handy, where you can stay aware of the things you need to get done during the day and then keep track of those accomplishments once the day comes to a close.

The act of crossing something off and reducing your to-do list will immediately boost your energy levels and make you feel excited for the next day, with one fewer chore to do. When you get home in the evening, go over the list and look for items that have been successfully completed. Cross those off and let them free your mind. You can cross them off with a different colored marker, such as red against black, or you can slash a huge *X* through each item to really make a statement. Do whatever energizes you the most.

TAKE YOUR DOG FOR A WALK

Studies have shown that walking a pet can improve energy levels and make you happier, and since pups especially can run and play with you, you can actually get your heart rate up quite a bit from all that movement and messing around. Give man's best friend some attention and love, allowing the bonding time to energize you and serve as a distraction from other anxiety-provoking thoughts, such as a work deadline or a big upcoming presentation.

So if you have a dog at home, play with him or her for a few minutes, or get some fresh air together. The fresh air will further boost energy levels. If you don't have a pet of your own, see if you can play with a neighbor's dog or accompany them on a walk. (Your neighbor may actually be super grateful for the help!)

WATCH THE SUN SET

Watching a sunset makes you reflect on the day and look forward to what's to come tomorrow. The beauty of a sunset can also make you feel more alive! Studies have shown that looking at beautiful, inspiring things can make us feel stimulated since they capture our attention.

Watching a sunset is also a great way to reflect in a natural setting, so you can try mindfulness meditation while watching the view. Just focus on the sunset as your objective. Research has shown that meditation can improve cognition, energy, and positive thinking, all of which contribute to greater well-being. (For more information on the benefits of meditation on increasing energy, look to the "Try Mindfulness Meditation" entry in Part 2.)

You can always share the sunset with someone else, if you prefer. In fact, depending on your personal preferences, viewing the sunset with a companion might further enhance energy by creating closeness and intimacy. Human connection is a great stimulant, and it makes us feel more alive with the world. So take a peek out your window to watch the sun go down, and enjoy the energy boost that will see you through the rest of the evening.

SWING A KETTLEBELL

If you're looking to gain some energy at the end of the day, try swinging a kettlebell! You know, those multicolored balls with handles that you see people using at the gym? Kettlebells are easy to use, and doing a few swings upon returning home can give you a major energy boost. A kettlebell swing works your glutes and lower body and requires a ton of physical and mental power, which means it will immediately crank your energy levels up, raise that heart rate, and burn some major calories in the process. In 5 minutes, you can do between 50 and 100 swings and burn up to 100 calories!

How to Swing a Kettlebell

1. With your feet hip width apart, place the kettlebell between your feet.
2. Squat down, grab the handles of the kettlebell, and swing it up and out in front of you.
3. Use your lower body weight to provide the force for the swing, and drive up from your heels. With arms straight and extended outward, let the kettlebell stop at about chest height before coming back down in the swing.
4. As the kettlebell descends downward, let it swing back through your legs before repeating.

Kettlebells are easy to store, and you can pick any weights that are most comfortable for you. For swings, you'll want something medium to heavy, as a kettlebell that's too light won't be as effective and could even be a bit unstable since you're swinging with so much force.

STARE AT YOUR PARTNER IN SILENCE

Sometimes you really don't need words to create an emotional effect and influence someone. Just looking into someone else's eyes in silence will do the trick. Here's what to do:

- Have your partner sit down in a chair across from you so you're facing each other.
- Reach for each other's hands and look into each other's eyes.
- Hold the gaze within this stillness.

What you're really doing here is peering into each other's souls and searching for your partner's "silent" inner thoughts. And doing this requires—and gives!—a lot of mental energy! You'll probably find yourself stimulated by the exchange and curious as to what the other person is thinking with such a powerful, steady look. By indulging in this curiosity, you're using a ton of energy to get the answers you're looking for. Plus, such a strong connection will create an intimate setting, where you'll feel closer to your partner. This intimacy will cause the release of the hormone oxytocin, called the love hormone, which gives you an energy boost and makes you feel tied to your partner.

PUT THE PHONE ON AIRPLANE MODE

If you're looking for an easy way to bump up your nighttime energy levels, try putting your phone on airplane mode for a few minutes! With a quick push of a button, you've silenced any distractions or anxiety-inducing emails and texts.

Of course, you can turn your phone back on again for the remainder of the evening—especially if you have someone who might need you for dinnertime—but taking 5 minutes just to be by yourself, enjoying liberation from any pressing matters, will give you an instant energy boost!

And if you don't want to shift modes, you can always leave your phone in a different room on silent so you won't be bothered by any dings or vibrations. Just find a way to disconnect from the world in favor of gaining some positive energy and clarity—which will help you recharge and refocus for the remaining hours ahead!

TURN DOWN THE THERMOSTAT!

It's time to crank that thermostat down, no matter the season! When you're too hot, you begin to feel light-headed and lethargic, which can slow you down and cause you to lose focus. Of course, don't set it so low that you're at risk of hypothermia. Studies have shown, though, that a cooler environment, something around 65°F, can provide a lift in energy and help increase cognitive function and concentration levels.

It's even better if you shiver a little bit, since shivering can provide a sudden hit of energy as well as burn calories and speed up your metabolism. The need to shiver also creates more heat and energy in the body in order to warm up the limbs, so it'll make your body feel more energized and agile. So if you are able to shiver for a few seconds, let yourself feel the chill and allow it to wake up your mind and body.

You can add more of a chill to the air by including a fan. That direct breeze can further enhance energy levels, and you can remove it if you become too cold. It's a great way to be in control of your cold therapy application, so plug in your fan and enjoy the breeze!

If the people you're with at home want the heat on or are getting too cold, you can change the thermostat in one room solely for 5 minutes, or put the fan close to your face so that only you're affected. You still need to be considerate of those around you, but be sure to let them know that it'll be for a short period of time and will likely energize them too!

LIGHT A CANDLE

If you're looking to stimulate your mind, body, and senses, light a candle! Candle scents are powerful and can create an energized outlook that lingers in your body and in the air for longer-lasting results. Candles come in a bunch of different aromas that all have been shown to provide significant energy benefits just through the power of scent! The popular scents in the following list have been shown to stimulate the mind and ease tension, helping you feel awake and in a positive mood:

- Peppermint
- Spearmint
- Lemongrass
- Rosemary
- Cinnamon
- Vanilla spice
- Eucalyptus
- Ginger
- Citrus flavors (such as grapefruit, orange, and lemon)

The scent will travel into your nose and circulate throughout the body, bringing energy to all areas. What's more, the visual aspect of a lighted, colorful candle amid dim lighting or a dark room will further stimulate your mind and body, providing an even heftier energy boost. Feel free to try out different scents and experiment to see which ones are most impactful for you.

LOOK AT A PHOTOGRAPH

You probably have photos, scrapbooks, and photo albums around your house, so take 5 minutes upon coming home in the evening to look at a few of them and let those feel-good emotions energize you with a renewed sense of vigor for life and the wonderful things and people within it. If you don't happen to have any tangible photos around, you can access them on your phone, on your social media pages, or in a folder on your desktop. You're likely to find a few smiling faces or silly moments somewhere that will lift your spirits.

This can be especially helpful after a long day or a draining week, and even more so if family or friends were away or you were stuck working late hours in isolation. Looking at photos is a friendly reminder of the energizing and positive aspects of life and how meaningful they are in shaping you and providing comfort and happiness.

FLOSS!

Feel refreshed and clean—ready to go! You may be surprised to hear this, but flossing your teeth when you're wrapping things up for the day can give you that burst of energy you need to take on the evening with a renewed sense of stamina. You know that icky sort of feeling in your mouth? It can be leftover residue from whatever you've been eating that day. By turning your attention to working through those crevices between your teeth, you stimulate your mind and create a more positive feeling within your body overall. Focusing on a specific task and paying keen attention to detail builds awareness in the mind, and that fresh feeling you get in your mouth will energize your spirits as well.

You can floss upon coming home before dinner for elevated energy levels, but don't forget to floss after dinner too! This will protect your teeth and lower your risk of gum disease, cavities, and any irritation to the mouth.

TAKE OUT OR WET YOUR CONTACTS

For those with contacts, you can probably all agree—when your contacts get dried out and smeared with gunk, it can make you lose concentration and focus and become lethargic. And when your eyes hurt or feel sleepy, it takes over your entire being, affecting your energy levels from head to toe. If you feel your eyes becoming weary, remove or wet your contacts if you can. Switching into glasses also gives your eyes a nice break!

If you have an evening commitment and don't want to change into your glasses just yet, consider changing or freshening up your contacts. You'll immediately feel more wide awake, comfortable, and ready to go out on the town. If you wear daily contacts, simply swap them out for a fresh version, or use an eye-drop solution to wet them. If you wear lenses that you need to change every two weeks or so, simply remove them and clean them in your contact solution, swirling them around a bit to get rid of any bacteria or germs, and then store them in their case. That said, if you use a contact solution with hydrogen peroxide, don't rinse and then reinsert your contacts right away. Instead opt for a gentler contact solution or eye drops instead.

PLANT SOMETHING

Studies have shown that gardening can give you a great energy boost and lead to more happiness. Spending time in nature is very grounding and healing, and as it's a symbol of birth and rebirth, it's a great way to feel rejuvenated! Here are a couple of ways to spend 5 minutes connecting with nature and greenery:

- Go to a local garden and plant something after work, or plant some seeds at home. There are many local communities, even in urban environments, and farmers' markets that provide access to growers and potted plants, where you can inquire more.
- If you have a terrace or space in the kitchen with sunlight, spend a few minutes creating a start for a plant's life. Just plant a few seeds for a flower or type of produce (like tomatoes, fresh herbs like basil and rosemary, or strawberries and blueberries). Doing so is very special, and you can watch your "babies" grow with time.

Let your own home garden, no matter the size or number of plants, energize you and give you something to nurture.

TRY GROUP THERAPY

Group therapy is where a group of people decides to work together to achieve a common goal that brings energy, relief, companionship, acceptance, and kindness. This type of therapy can be energizing when you think about working toward meeting those desired goals and experience the positivity that the group can provide. You can look within your community for group therapy opportunities, search online for events and organizations, or just form one on your own! You can work to connect with a group of strangers or even just a few close acquaintances and friends who would want to connect regularly and give each other energy at the end of the day. Here are a few group therapy options to choose from:

- **Meditation group therapy:** Here you can practice mindfulness meditation in a group setting and look to others for help in boosting energy and honing your skills. You can do breath work, do a guided meditation with a leader in the community, or practice meditation through sound therapy, which may use gongs, ocean sounds, or meditation music. You can also try meditation in silence—where you're simply relying on the group for that reboot in mindset and energy.
- **Yoga group therapy:** Similar to meditation but with more movement, this is a great way to stick with yoga and stretching, as there

are others to hold you accountable and act as a resource that provides energy. You might go through a flow of poses, where each person takes turns choosing a position, or have a leader who decides for the group and guides everyone along the energizing journey.

- **Creative art as group therapy:** You can gather a team or join a group of people who enjoy using art as a way to boost energy and creativity. This can be a book club, a drawing or painting club, a dance club, a knitting club—anything that works toward focusing on art and expression as a way to create more vibrancy in your life and stimulate the senses.

Group therapy offers a true support system, so you'll feel energized and connected to others.

WASH THE DISHES

You might think that washing the dishes sounds like a drag, but it's actually a great way to boost your energy levels! The act of cleaning itself gets the body and mind working, which puts your focus back on track with a task at hand that's automatic, requiring little thought. So in a way, it's pretty meditative too.

In addition, studies have shown that a neat and tidy place can make you feel more energized in general, so sorting out the dishes and clearing the kitchen will make you feel in control of your surroundings and alert.

And the water splashing on your hands will further improve energy, as cool water can serve as an immediate refresher! If you don't have any dishes to wash, just take a clean utensil or bowl and give it a scrub. It'll be just as beneficial as if it were actually dirty.

DO TABATA

Tabata is a type of workout that consists of a circuit, where you're doing 20 seconds of an activity and taking 10 seconds off, alternating for a whole 4 minutes. The catch is you need to give the activity your all in those 20 seconds, so you're in dire need of that break. You should be out of breath, your heart should be beating outside your chest, and you should be breaking a sweat—even in that short amount of time. The good news is that this short, 4-minute activity will give you some serious energy and spike your heart rate, helping you burn major calories and tone and strengthen your muscles. Here are a few common moves associated with tabata training:

- **Burpees:** This intense move will energize you in a second (literally!). You throw your body down on the ground and do a full push-up, then simply use the force of your body to push yourself up from the ground and jump back up with your arms overhead. Repeat this again to a do a few sets of burpees at once.
- **Mountain climbers:** Here you'll go into plank on the ground by placing your palms on the floor underneath your shoulders, pointing your toes toward the floor, and keeping your body aligned, straight, and facing the ground. Keep your back flat and straight with your butt down, and run your legs inward toward your hands, as though you're sprinting. To make this move more

difficult, cross your legs inward (with the opposite knee to hand) for cross-body mountain climbers or outward with each knee for wide mountain climbers.

- **Skaters:** These are great for getting some energizing cardio without too much pressure on joints (but if you have knee troubles, be careful). You skate from side to side, arms straight out, with the opposite arm reaching toward the floor with each skate. To skate, simply jump to the left with your left knee bent and shoot your right leg behind you, as if you were going to curtsy. Then switch to the right side with your left leg shooting out. Alternate from side to side.
- **Tuck jumps:** Be careful if you have bad knees, as tuck jumps put a lot of pressure on them, but if you're in the clear, tuck jumps provide a major burst of energy. To tuck your knees, jump up and bring your knees upward with you, as if you are touching your knees with your hands. Then gently land on the ground with your feet planted and legs straight, back to a standing position.

Tabata exercises spike your heart rate for a major energy boost, and they burn lots of calories!

LIFT WEIGHTS

Lifting weights provides greater energy since exercising can boost blood flow, circulation, and strength in the body, and keeping the proper form requires concentration. You wouldn't want to drop those weights! By lifting and counting reps for 5 minutes, you'll bring energy to both your body and mind, and it'll have longer-lasting effects as well! You'll actually feel stimulated for a few more hours to come.

That being said, don't start picking up those weights at 10 p.m. You don't want to be too stimulated so close to bedtime, since it can prevent you from falling asleep and make it challenging to enjoy those energizing benefits. (Without enough sleep, you'll wake up even more sluggish than usual.) Think backward: what time do you want to get into bed? Give yourself 2 hours beforehand to finish up with those weights and allow yourself to power down into sleep mode right on schedule.

PICK OUT YOUR OUTFIT FOR TOMORROW

Spare 5 minutes in the evening to lay out your clothes for the next day. Getting yourself organized the night before invigorates you, and you'll feel more eager to get started the following day and tackle whatever's on your plate. Any way to save time and feel confident in your skin will make you have more energy, as mood and energy are intertwined. Plus, it can actually be fun!

Try on different shirts, pants, and shoes, and even play around with accessories, such as a necklace, ring, tie, or belt. You can even take some time to relish in your dapper appearance and put on a little fashion show for yourself (or your kids, as they might want to join in too!).

And the benefits will carry over to the next day! Feeling great about the outfit you're in (and not having to worry about what you're going to wear!) will immediately give you a spring in your step when you walk out the front door and start a new day.

SCRUB YOURSELF WITH A LOOFAH

Hop in the shower and give yourself a good exfoliation by scrubbing with a loofah and shower gel. Applying abrasion to the skin will invigorate your mind and body—and it'll bring softness and rejuvenation to your skin. What's more, the shower itself will make you feel more energized and awake after a long day, as water on the skin can instantly perk you up and wipe out your fatigue.

For an even greater boost, find a shower gel with a smell that arouses and energizes your senses. A few options might be vanilla and cinnamon, citrus (such as lemon, grapefruit, or mandarin), eucalyptus and "spa" aromas, and fresh tropical fruits (such as pineapple, mango, or coconut).

Don't scrub so hard that you damage your skin or feel pain, though. Use just enough pressure so you can feel yourself removing those dry, rough patches in favor of clean, fresh ones—and enjoy the energy boost!

TAKE OUT THE TRASH

Get your legs moving with a trip to the chute or garage! Taking out the trash is an easy, energy-boosting activity that you have to do anyway, right? This chore requires movement, which increases blood flow and circulation throughout the body, making you feel more energized. And it removes clutter, which itself can drain energy and make you feel lethargic and stressed. Make a plan to go from room to room, emptying wastebaskets and compiling a big load of trash to then take out.

For a little added work, take your recyclable items out too! This way, you'll need to take two trips, and the longer you're on your feet, the more energy you'll have. And you can even make a trip out to the compost pile with compostable items for a few extra steps—not to mention you're further helping the planet too! If you hate taking out the trash, turn on some music as a distraction. The music will further energize you and put you in a fantastic mood.

MAKE A RANDOM PLAN AFTER WORK

Instead of heading home at the end of the day, take a detour and do something spontaneous and unexpected! The idea of spontaneity is huge in creating energy and stimulation, as it gets your mind and body excited about something out of the ordinary. Here are a few suggestions:

- Call up a friend or family member to get dinner or drinks, catch a movie or comedy show, or join you on a shopping trip. You can even surprise someone with tickets or a reservation if you know that he or she will be open to the last-minute plan.
- Get a workout in by popping into a class. If you don't have any gear on hand, head home first and book a later class. Or you can stash a set of workout clothes in your office each week to have on hand, just in case you're up for an evening spin or yoga session.
- Give yourself some downtime outside the home. Head to the park after work and relax on a bench for a bit. Or pick up a book at a local bookstore and enjoy a cup of tea with a good read for an hour or so before heading home.
- Take a different commute on your way back home. There's a great opportunity to indulge in new sights, sounds, and aspects of beauty by taking another path home. Whether you're walking,

driving, taking mass transit, or cycling, get off at a different stop or take a detour and explore a new block. The novelty of the situation will energize you and provide more stimulation and intrigue, and it helps break up the normalcy of the workday. This time alone will also help you separate from the world and its pressing matters, which can drain you.

Spontaneity helps shake things up, providing unexpected energy and excitement for something that's soon to come!

DO WORK YOU'VE BEEN PUTTING OFF

You know that last set of papers you've needed to get through for the past month? Or the files you've been meaning to clear from your desktop or office cabinet? Spend a few minutes in the evening, once the craziness of the day has ended, to get this stuff off your desk—and off your to-do list! Finishing up these chores that you've been putting off will actually provide a boost in energy, as you'll feel great once they're finally completed.

After all, when you are stuck with tasks that never seem to get done and are just hanging over your head, it can make you feel stressed, lethargic, and unmotivated to make moves and check them off your list. And unfortunately, once there's no longer a sense of urgency, the determination you once had to get these things taken care of can waver. So take just 5 minutes to work in bits and pieces to tackle these projects—and reap the energizing benefits that come with the understanding that you're getting closer and closer to meeting your goals.

PLAY A GAME OF CARDS

There's nothing like a game of cards to boost your mental thinking and provide a burst of energy. Anything that requires attention to detail, memory, and concentration will be taxing on the brain, and a game of cards, which calls for all of these actions, will surely wake you up. The act of competing, even if you're just playing alone, is exciting and energizing, as it puts you on a mission to win. Plus, it's fun!

Ask your significant other or children to play a round or two with you, or if you're alone, head online and search for a card game site. There are many chats you can enter where you're playing with other people around the world. No matter the crowd or participants, you'll still get the energizing benefits and find something pleasurable to engage in after a long day.

TRY A NEW FOOD FOR DINNER

Looking to spice things up? Mix up your dinner routine and try something new! When you shock your body and mind with novelty, especially in the form of food, you'll find yourself experiencing a major energy boost. Why? Well, food directly energizes the senses and brings your attention to flavors and textures. And this is important for new foods especially, since eating them can cause your taste buds to perk up even more as you haven't tried them before. Plus, since food is fuel, it immediately reboots the system and gets you thinking and mobile again. Here are a few ways to surprise your taste buds and get an energy boost at the end of the day:

- Add new spices, herbs, marinades, or sauces to your dish. These will change the flavors of the meal, providing a new gastronomic adventure for greater energy.
- Try a different protein. If you always go for chicken, try steak, short ribs, or fish. You can even replicate recipes you're used to but change the main protein for something different that's still within your comfort zone and pantry.
- Pick something up from outdoors or a restaurant. If you're always cooking in the kitchen, change things up by treating yourself and your close ones to a delicious meal outdoors for something new that can't necessarily be created at home.

- Pair your food with a new beverage that complements the food's flavors and textures. Do you usually opt for a glass of Merlot? Or is water your go-to during week nights? Change things up by choosing a cocktail, a different wine, a beer, or a flavored water or juice that might bring out the notes in the dish better and surprise your taste buds. You'll get a pop of energy in your mouth that'll carry over to your mind and body.

Make a plan to try at least one new food a week, whether it's through a swap in spice or sauce or a whole recipe you've had your eye on.

ICE YOUR MUSCLES

Have you heard of ice therapy? All you have to do is take 5 minutes to ice your thighs, neck, shoulders, or back, which will wake you up, release tension, and improve your blood flow and circulation. Plus, if you do this on a regular basis, you'll better prevent chronic pain or fatigue that can happen from overworked, tired muscles.

So put just a few ice cubes in a plastic bag, or use an ice pack from your local drugstore. Wear a light shirt or put the ice pack with a paper towel around it on your skin. You don't want to put it directly on your skin if it's too cold, but you do want to be able to feel the chill and get the energizing benefits you need.

HAVE A LITTLE BIT OF ICE CREAM

In need of some energy at the end of the day? Don't be afraid to splurge on a little bit of ice cream! As ice cream has sugar, it increases dopamine, a hormone associated with feel-good emotions, which can make you feel energized and happy. It's an instant wake-up call to your mouth, mind, and body. Plus, it tastes yummy!

As long as you make sure to practice proper portion control, ice cream is the perfect dessert. If you're worried, just look at the label and search for lower-calorie and higher-protein ice cream options, such as Halo Top or Yasso frozen Greek yogurt, which are widely available and delicious! And as long as you're having only a quick snack, you probably won't polish off that whole pint either.

Don't choose an ice cream that contains caffeine—like coffee, chocolate, or mocha—if you're worried about not being able to fall asleep at night. If these are your favorites, have this evening snack earlier, allowing yourself enough time to get sleepy for bed. Instead try these:

- Lemon sorbet
- Lavender
- Chamomile
- Vanilla bean
- Strawberry shortcake

Just this little serving of ice cream will be enough to give you some energy without going overboard. And as sugar can lead to a crash later on, it won't be *so* bad if you end up a bit fatigued a few hours after. It might even be easier to fall asleep when you *want* to be fatigued.

INDEX

Accomplishment, sharing, 121

Activity, staying on your feet, 17–18

Adventure, sharing, 122

Afternoon, energizing, 183–234

biting your tongue, 224

bobbing your head to a song, 226

chatting with coworker, 193

cleaning your glasses, 208–9

doing a wall sit, 233–34

doing squats, 194–95

drinking cold water, 192

eating handful of nuts, 196–97

eating some fruit, 199–200

eating something salty, 211–12

holding your breath, 203

inhaling essential oils, 190–91

jumping rope, 229

looking up restaurant menu, 206

making yes/meh list, 231–32

massaging yourself, 220

patting someone else on the shoulder, 221

patting yourself on the back, 219

pinching yourself, 201

practicing kanban, 222–23

practicing power pose, 188–89

rotating your wrists, 218

scratching your back, 210

splashing cool water on face, 187

squeezing stress ball, 225

sticking your head out window, 228

stretching/opening up your hips, 215–16

stretching your ankles, 204

stretching your back, 29–30, 213–14

taking call and pacing, 217

taking the stairs, 184–85

texting a friend, 207

walking briskly, 186

washing your hands, 202

wearing red, 230

whistling and, 227

writing haiku, 198

Airplane mode, putting phone on, 254

Alarm, setting to a song, 149

Ankles, stretching, 204

Apple cider vinegar, drinking, 152

Arms, stretching, 30

Back, scratching, 210

Back, stretching, 29–30, 213–14

Ball (stress), squeezing, 225

Bathroom, using, 181

Bed, making, 180
Biting your tongue, 224
Breathing
deep breath, 24
effects of, 24
getting fresh air, 33
holding your breath, 203
inhaling essential oils,
  190–91
sniffing ginger, 112–13
wake-up exercise, 134
Brushing your teeth, 159
Burpees, tabata training,
  264

Candle, lighting, 256
Cards, playing game of, 273
Change
learning new words, 84
trying new food for dinner,
  274–75
trying something new, 25
Chocolate (dark), indulging
  in, 245
Cleaning
the dishes, 263
something in your home,
  239
tidying your house and,
  37–38
your ears, 169
your face, 247
your glasses, 208–9

your hands, 202
yourself with loofa, 268
Clothing
donating to charity, 44
picking outfit for tomorrow,
  267
putting away, 37
wearing red, 230
Cloud art, looking for, 72
Coffee, 142–43, 174
Cologne, spraying, 170
Coloring, 107
Commute, enjoying, 162–63
Complimenting yourself,
  42–43
Contacts, taking out or
  wetting, 259
Coworker, chatting with,
  193
Creative art, as group
  therapy, 262

Dancing, 17, 53, 236
Daydreaming, 68–69
Dental care. See Oral care
Dining. See Food/eating
Dishes, washing, 263
Dog, walking, 249
Doodling, 88
Dream list, making, 36
Drinking
apple cider vinegar, 152
coffee, 142–43

cold water, 192
green juice, 150–51
kombucha, 179
matcha, 168
smoothies, 172–73
warm water and lemon, 136
water, 48, 192
wine, 73

Ears, cleaning, 169
Eating. See Food/eating
Espresso beans, eating, 174
Essential oils, inhaling,
  190–91
Evening, energizing,
  235–78
cleaning something in
  home, 239
crossing off your to-do list,
  248
dancing when making din-
  ner, 236
dining with good company,
  243
doing tabata, 264–65
doing work you've put off,
  272
eating healthy meal,
  237–38
flossing your teeth, 258
group therapy, 261–62
having little bit of ice cream,
  277–78

icing your muscles, 276
indulging in dark chocolate, 245
lifting weights, 266
lighting a candle, 256
looking at photo(s), 257
making random plan after work, 270–71
making time for sex, 240–41
picking outfit for tomorrow, 267
planting something, 260
playing card game, 273
prepping for tomorrow, 242
putting phone on airplane mode, 254
scrubbing with loofa, 268
staring at partner in silence, 253
swinging kettlebell(s), 251–52
taking out or wetting contacts, 259
taking out trash, 269
trying new food for dinner, 274–75
turning down thermostat, 255
using foam roller on muscles, 246
walking dog, 249
washing the dishes, 263

washing your face, 247
watching favorite TV show, 244
watching sunset, 250
Excitement, 101
Exercise. See also Stretching; Yoga, benefits and poses
class, booking, 156
doing a plank, 115–16
doing a wall sit, 233–34
HIIT workout, 26
icing your muscles, 276
jumping jacks, 157
lifting weights, 266
massage after. See Massage
squats, 194–95
swinging kettlebell(s), 251–52
tabata training, 264–65
taking the stairs, 184–85
wake-up routine (5-minute), 144
walking briskly, 186
walking your dog, 249
Eyes
cleaning your glasses, 208–9
taking out or wetting contacts, 259
wetting, 106

Face, splashing cool water on, 187
Face, washing, 247
Fear, thinking of something that scares you, 148
Feet, stretching, 177–78
Flossing your teeth, 258
Food/eating. See also Drinking
apple, 167
banana, 161
cooking and, 49
dancing when making dinner, 236
dark chocolate, 245
dining with good company, 243
ditching sugar, 57–58
eating healthy meal, 237–38
eating mindfully, 55–56, 196–97
energizing dinner dishes, 237–38
espresso beans, 174
fruit, 199–200
getting enough iron, 59–60
grapefruit, 164
Greek yogurt, 153
ice cream, 277–78
looking up restaurant menu, 206

lox, 154
mealtime with family, 50
morning protein power-up, 139–40
nuts, 196–97
salty snacks, 211–12
snacks to stock, 21–22
sniffing ginger, 112–13
something fishy, 110–11
starting dinner, 182
taking probiotics, 62–63
trying new food for dinner, 274–75
washing dishes after, 263
whole grains, 45–46
Forgiving yourself, 74
Fruit, eating, 199–200

Gardening, planting something, 260
Gargling with water, 160
Ginger, sniffing, 112–13
Giving. See also Gratitude; Love
donating to charity, 44
sharing an accomplishment, 121
sharing an adventure, 122
Glasses, cleaning, 208–9
Goal, setting. See also To-do list, making
Goals, setting, 125, 126

Good qualities, getting feedback on, 131
Grapefruit, eating, 164
Gratitude. See also Giving; Love
complimenting yourself, 42–43
keeping gratitude journal, 19–20
patting someone else on the shoulder, 221
sharing what you love about someone, 96
Group therapy, 261–62
Gum, chewing peppermint, 86

Haiku, writing, 198
Hair, fixing, 135
Hair, pulling, 100
Hands, washing, 202
Hips, stretching/opening up, 215–16
Hobby, new, 40, 126
Home
cleaning something in, 239
taking out trash, 269
tidying up, 37–38
turning down thermostat, 255
washing the dishes, 263
Humor, 27
Hypnosis, self-, 94–95

Ice cream, having little bit of, 277–78
Icing your muscles, 276
Indulging
in dark chocolate, 245
in something, 75
in a talent, 128
in wishful thinking, 176
Instrument, playing, 109
Intention, setting positive, 137
Iron, getting enough, 59–60

Jumping jacks, doing, 157
Jumping rope, 229

Kanban, practicing, 222–23
Kettlebells, swinging, 251–52
Kissing someone, 175
Knitting, 108
Kombucha, sipping, 179

Laughter, 27
Legs, stretching, 30, 118, 177–78, 204–5
Life, energizing, 15–75
being open to love, 53–54
breathing deeply, 24
channeling inner yogi, 66–67. See also Yoga, benefits and poses

complimenting yourself, 42–43
considering "what if" scenario, 68–69
cooking, 49
ditching sugar, 57–58
donating to charity, 44
drinking wine, 73
eating mindfully, 55–56
eating whole grains, 45–46
eating with family, 50
eliminating toxins, 51–52
embracing water, 47
forgiving yourself, 74
getting enough iron, 59–60
getting outside, fresh air, 32–33
HIIT workout, 26
indulging in something, 75
keeping gratitude journal, 19–20
looking for cloud art, 72
making dream list, 36
making someone laugh, 27
meditating, 34–35
music and, 23
not sweating small stuff, 61
practicing new hobby, 40
prebiotics and, 64–65
probiotics and, 62–63
reading newspaper, 39
reading poetry, 31

saying "I love you" daily, 16
singing loud and proud, 41
smiling for, 28
snacks for, 21–22
staying hydrated, 48
staying on your feet, 17–18
stretching for, 29–30
taking photo of your pet, 71
tidying up, 37–38
touching someone gently, 70
trying something new, 25
Lifting weights, 266
Lighting a candle, 256
Loofa, scrubbing self with, 268
Love. See also Giving; Gratitude
forgiving yourself, 74
kissing someone, 175
listing five things you love about yourself, 102–3
making time for sex, 240–41
openness to, tips, 53–54
patting someone else on the shoulder, 221
saying "I love you" daily, 16
self-, 42–43, 219
sharing what you love about someone, 96
staring at partner in silence, 253

touching someone gently, 70
Lox, eating, 154

Magazine (new), reading, 129–30
Mailbox, checking, 158
Massage
giving yourself one, 220
pulling your hair and, 100
rubbing your temples, 89
using foam roller, 246
Matcha, drinking shot of, 168
Meals. See Food/eating
Meditation. See also Yoga
group therapy, 261
mindfulness, 81–82
practicing, 34–35
Meh/yes list, making, 231–32
Menu (restaurant), looking up, 206
Mind, energizing, 77–131. See also Meditation; Yoga, benefits and poses
asking someone to list your good qualities, 131
chewing peppermint gum, 86
coloring and, 107
connecting with old friend, 124

conversing with a stranger, 85

doodling and, 88

eating something fishy, 110–11

getting excited, 101

indulging in a talent, 128

knitting and, 108

learning new words, 84

listing five things you love about yourself, 102–3

looking in mirror, 123

playing an instrument, 109

playing home movie, 119

positive affirmation for, 91

pulling your hair, 100

reading new magazine, 129–30

reciting powerful words, 90

rubbing your temples, 89

screaming and, 99

self-hypnosis for, 94–95

setting goals, 125, 126

sharing an accomplishment, 121

sharing an adventure, 122

sharing what you love about someone, 96

snapping your fingers, 98

sniffing ginger, 112–13

social media for, 104, 105

solving puzzles, 83

taking online quiz, 79–80

thinking positively, 78

touching your toes, 118

visualization technique for, 92–93

wetting your eyes, 106

working on bad habit, 127

writing personal letter, 97

Mindful eating, 55–56, 196–97

Mindfulness meditation, 81–82

Mirror, looking in, 123

Morning, energizing, 133–82

booking exercise class, 156

brushing your teeth, 159

checking mailbox, 158

cleaning your ears, 169

doing jumping jacks, 157

drinking coffee, 142–43

drinking green juice, 150–51

drinking shot of apple cider vinegar, 152

drinking shot of matcha, 168

drinking smoothies, 172–73

drinking water and lemon, 136

eating a banana, 161

eating an apple, 167

eating espresso beans, 174

eating grapefruit, 164

eating Greek yogurt, 153

eating lox, 154

enjoying commute, 162–63

fixing your hair, 135

gargling with water, 160

getting heart rate up, 144

indulging in wishful thinking, 176

kissing someone, 175

making plans, 155

making to-do list, 147

making your bed, 180

protein power-up for, 139–40

saying "Good morning," 141

setting alarm to a song, 149

setting positive intention, 137

showering, 146

sipping kombucha, 179

snapping a selfie, 171

spraying perfume/cologne, 170

starting dinner, 182

stretching your feet, 177–78

stretching your neck, 136

taking photo of outdoors, 165

thinking of something that scares you, 148

using the restroom, 181

wake-up breathing exercise, 134
watering plants, 166
winking at yourself, 145
Mountain climbers, tabata training, 264–65
Muscles, icing, 276
Muscles, working out/ stretching. See Exercise; Stretching
Music
bobbing your head to, 226
listening to, enjoying, 23
playing an instrument, 109
setting alarm to a song, 149
singing loud and proud, 41

Neck, stretching, 29, 138
Newspaper, reading, 39
New things, trying, 25
Nuts, eating, 196–97

Oils, essential, inhaling, 190–91
Oral care
brushing your teeth, 159
flossing, 258
gargling with water, 160
Outdoors
energizing effect of, 32–33
getting fresh air, 33
looking for cloud art, 72

sticking your head out window, 228
taking photo of, 165

Patting yourself on the back, 219
Peppermint, 86, 159, 160, 190
Perfume, spraying, 170
Pets
being open to love from, 53
taking photo of, 71
walking dog, 249
Phone, putting on airplane mode, 254
Photos
looking at, 54, 257
of outdoors, taking, 165
selfies, 171
of your pet, taking, 71
Pinching yourself, 201
Plans, making, 155
Planting something, 260
Plants, watering, 166
Playing card game, 273
Poetry, 31, 198
Positivity
positive affirmation, 91
positive thinking, 78
setting intention for, 137
Power pose, practicing, 188–89
Prebiotics, 64–65

Prepping for tomorrow, 242
Probiotics, 62–63
Productivity and time management. See also Work
crossing off to-do list, 248
doing work you've put off, 272
making plans, 155
making to-do list, 147
making yes/meh list, 231–32
practicing kanban, 222–23
prepping for tomorrow, 242
setting goals, 125, 126
setting positive intention, 137
Pulling your hair, 100
Puzzles, solving, 83

Quiz, taking, 79–80

Reading
new magazine, 129–30
newspaper, 39
poetry, 31
Red, wearing, 230
Restaurant menu, looking up, 206
Restroom, using, 181

Salty snacks, eating, 211–12
Scratching your back, 210
Screaming, 99

Selfie, taking, 171
Sex, making time for, 240–41. *See also* Love
Showering, 146
Silence, staring at partner in, 253
Skaters, tabata training, 265
Small stuff, not sweating, 61
Smoothies, 172–73
Snacks for energy, 21–22, 211–12. *See also* Food/eating
Snapping your fingers, 98
Sniffing ginger, 112–13
Social media, energizing your mind, 104, 105
Speaking
conversing with a stranger, 85
with coworker, 193
reciting powerful words, 90
saying "Good morning," 141
saying "I love you" daily, 16
sharing an accomplishment, 121
sharing what you love about someone, 96
taking call and pacing, 217
Squats, doing, 194–95
Squeezing stress ball, 225
Stairs, taking, 184–85

Staring at partner in silence, 253
Stress ball, squeezing, 225
Stretching
ankles, 204–5
arms, 30
back, 29–30, 213–14
benefits of, 29
feet, 177–78
hips, 215–16
legs, 30, 118, 177–78, 204–5
neck, 29, 138
touching your toes, 118
wrists, 218
yoga group therapy, 261–62
yoga poses, 66–67, 87, 114, 115–16, 117, 120
Sugar, ditching, 57–58
Sunset, watching, 250

Tabata training, 264–65
Talent, indulging in, 128
Talking. *See* Speaking
Temperature, turning down, 255
Temples, rubbing, 89
Texting a friend, 207
Thermostat, turning down, 255
Tidying up, 37–38

Time management. *See* Productivity and time management
To-do list
crossing off, 248
making, 147
Tongue, biting, 224
Touching others, 70, 221
Toxins, eliminating, 51–52
Trash, taking out, 269
Tuck jumps, tabata training, 265
TV and videos
playing home movie, 119
watching favorite TV show, 244

Videos (home), playing, 119
Visualization technique, 92–93

Walking briskly, 186
Walking dog, 249
Wall squat/sit, 233–34
Washing. *See* Cleaning
Water
cold, drinking, 192
cool, splashing on face, 187
embracing, enjoying, 47
gargling with, 160
staying hydrated, 48
watering plants, 166
Wearing red, 230

Weights, lifting, 266
"What if" scenario, considering, 68–69
Whistling, 227
Window, sticking your head out, 228
Wine, pouring glass of, 73
Winking at yourself, 145
Wishful thinking, indulging in, 176
Words, learning new, 84
Work. *See also* Productivity and time management
chatting with coworker, 193
doing what you've put off, 272
enjoying commute, 162–63
making random plan after, 270–71
Wrists, rotating, 218
Writing
haiku, 198
keeping gratitude journal, 19–20
listing five things you love about yourself, 102–3
making dream list, 36
personal letter, 97
texting a friend, 207
to-do list, 147

Yes/meh list, making, 231–32

Yoga, benefits and poses, 66–67, 87, 114, 115–16, 117, 120
Yoga group therapy, 261–62
Yogurt, Greek, 153

ABOUT THE AUTHOR

Isadora Baum is a freelance writer and certified health coach who loves trying new health foods; coaching clients toward achieving their goals; and living her life with a curious, creative energy. She writes for *Bustle*, *Shape*, *Men's Health*, *Women's Health*, *PopSugar*, *Health*, *Reader's Digest*, *Runner's World*, *Prevention*, and more. She can't resist a sample, a margarita, a HIIT class, a challenge or adventure, or an easy laugh. You can learn more about her on her website, IsadoraBaum.com.